FOLLOW
THE
PROCESS

BOOK
POWER
PUBLISHING

DETROIT, MICHIGAN

FOLLOW THE PROCESS
A STORY OF PERSEVERANCE, PURPOSE AND PASSING THE TORCH

Published in the United States by Book Power Publishing, an imprint of Niyah Press, Detroit, Michigan.

www.bookpowerpublishing.com

Book Power Publishing books may be purchased for educational, business, or sales promotional use.

For bulk sales, contact the author: **drgwen.thornton.author@gmail.com**

First Edition

PRINTED IN THE UNITED STATES OF AMERICA.

ISBN:
978-1-964965-20-8 **hardback**
978-1-964965-21-5 **paperback**
978-1-964965-22-2 **ebook**

www.bookpowerpublishing.com

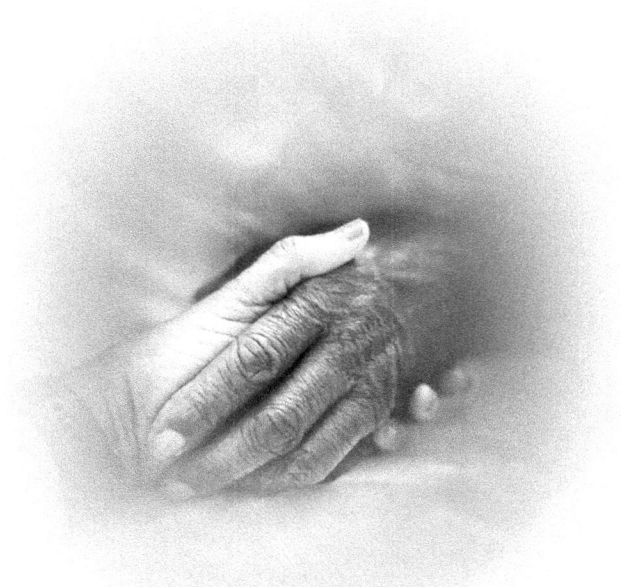

FOLLOW
THE
PROCESS

A STORY OF PERSEVERANCE, PURPOSE AND PASSING THE TORCH

Dr. GWENDOLYN BROWN THORNTON

ADVANCED PRAISE

My Cousin Gwen's beautiful book stands as a powerful reminder of how all of our lives are shaped by a complex combination of genetics, cultures, communities and living people of courage, faith and love. At the same time her story serves as a reminder of the God-given freedom we have to make decisions which shape and reshape our lives and the lives of those around us.

Personally, this book invokes memories of what it was like to enjoy a childhood in a sheltering, nurturing Black community! To read this is to relive such nurturing and calls you to not just feel it anew but to also want to share it with a new generation.

— *Rev. Larry C. Green, Sr.*
Pastor Emeritus (2013)
Grace Baptist Church
Waterbury, Connecticut

CONTENTS

Advanced Praise..   v

Dedication   ix

Foreword..   xi

Preface   xiii

Introduction: Born of a Village, Bound by Legacy........................   xv

CHAPTER 1

The Early Years of Gwendolyn (Gwen) Brown   1

CHAPTER 2

The Roots of My Ancestrial Village Legacy   11

CHAPTER 3

Alice and Randolph Brown – Safe Haven Sanctuary Covered

in Favor: 35

CHAPTER 4

Union Baptist: Our Village's Sacred Home   47

CHAPTER 5

Embarking on a Lifelong Odyssey of Learning.......................   57

CHAPTER 6

Navigating the Uncharted Waters of Independence and

Responsibility   83

CHAPTER 7

My Journey Through Pain and Growth...................................   89

CHAPTER 9

Pain, Perseverance, and Strength   107

CHAPTER 11

A Dream Realized: My Journey to The Heart of Africa 133

CHAPTER 12

Purpose, Service, and Strength 141

CHAPTER 13

Walking Through Pain With Purpose 149

CHAPTER 14

Stepping into Divine Purpose 155

CHAPTER 15

A Legacy of Purpose: Transforming Lives Through Service 161

CHAPTER 16

Walking In Divine Order: Trusting God's Plan Through Life's
Transition 177

CHAPTER 17

Follow the Process 183

Epilogue: The Seeds I Carried: A Legacy in Bloom 187

About the Author 197

DEDICATION

To my ancestors, known and unnamed, who dreamed beyond bondage and believed in a future they would never see—your footsteps guide mine. This memoir is shaped by your presence, lifted by your prayers, and rooted in our shared legacy. May these pages honor the lives you lived, the sacrifices you made, and the light you passed down. I offer heartfelt gratitude to all. To my ancestors and all those whose names may be forgotten but whose spirits remain etched in my soul. You laid the foundation with love, labor, and prayer.

To my parents, whose sacrifices and wisdom shaped my path.

To my son, whose presence gave my journey deeper meaning, and whose words now carry my story forward with grace and truth.

To the village—mentors, elders, friends, and faith companions—who lifted me when I was weary, guided me when I was uncertain, and celebrated me when I triumphed.

To every student who dared to dream beyond circumstance, and every reader who seeks healing through story—may these pages be a light on your path.

And to the God who never left my side, even when the road was steep and the night was long.

"I am because we are, and since we are, therefore I am."
— Ubuntu proverb

This book is for you.
This legacy is ours.
And the torch still burns.

FOREWORD

As the proud son of Dr. Gwendolyn Brown Thornton—and the great-great-grandson of Ida Carter and William Albert Christian—I offer this foreword as both tribute and testimony. This book is not meant to be read with the eyes alone, but embraced by the heart, mind, and spirit.

My mother's journey is one of faith, fortitude, and fierce love. It traces the history of three families—Christian, Carter, and Brown—united in legacy and rooted in values that transcend generations. Her story carries you through personal and collective trials: navigating family dynamics, growing up during the Civil Rights movement, and confronting a world that often treated Black lives as second-class.

She raised me as a single mother, leaning on the shoulders of mentors and the strength of "the village." She called on elders and community men to guide me from boyhood to manhood, all while balancing work, education, caregiving, and service. Her sacrifices were quiet but profound—always thinking of others' well-being before her own.

From a one-room schoolhouse in New Kent to becoming Department Chair of Social Work at Virginia State University, she walked with purpose, leaning on the morals instilled in her from childhood. Her journey is etched in these pages—in the smiles and joys, the pain and perseverance, the blessings and breakthroughs.

This book reveals how, when one door closed, God opened another— leading her to build a strong Social Work program and leave behind a roadmap for students to follow. She reminds us to set aside material things and focus on what truly matters: faith, family, self, and education.

Her words will inspire, enlighten, and touch your soul. They carry the prayers of our ancestors and the love of the village that still walks with us. A torch was passed to her, and now she passes it again. It's up to this generation to keep it lit.

And in her words: "Follow God, follow your spirit, and most of all... FOLLOW THE PROCESS!"

Arthur 'LeDon' Thornton

PREFACE

Telling the stories that shaped me so others may rise—because memory is a gift, truth is a torch, and every lived experience holds the power to illuminate someone else's path. Through the echo of my ancestors, the lessons of my struggles, and the quiet grace of my faith, I share not only where I've been, but what it means to keep walking forward for those yet to come.

BORN OF A VILLAGE, BOUND BY LEGACY

Before I knew the world, I knew Quinton, my ancestral village nestled in the heart of Virginia, where dirt roads carried both the dust of history and the dreams of tomorrow. In that sacred soil, where elders waved from porches and Sunday meals lasted well into the evening, my story began. In that cradle of faith and family, my roots took hold.

Quinton was more than a place on a map. It was a heartbeat and a sanctuary of love, shaped by generations who worked with their hands and prayed with their whole hearts. Everything about the land, the rhythm of humming bees in summer gardens, the clang of church bells echoing through the pines, the shrieks of cousins chasing fireflies at twilight, offered lessons no textbook could teach but every soul understood.

My parents were born of this village soil and baptized by its sacred rhythms. They raised me with a reverence for community and a humility that settled gently into the spirit like evening dew. They passed down not just stories, but a code of living. This included a devotion to service, the strength to endure sorrow with dignity, and the grace to forgive when forgiveness felt like sacrifice. I watched them live this truth daily. Their quiet labor of love and unspoken strength rose up in times of need.

In Quinton, every elder was a teacher, every neighbor a mirror reflecting our growth. We celebrated together, mourned together, and stood shoulder to shoulder when the world outside our village forgot our names.

The village held our history like sacred scripture—preserved in tales whispered on porches at dusk, in names etched into worn hymnals, in patchwork quilts stitched with stories only the heart could read. Faith was not a distant idea but a living force, woven into the cooking, the caregiving, and the communal prayers that lifted us over hard times. Though modest in size, Quinton carried the weight of generations— each adding their prayer, their struggle, their celebration to our shared legacy with reverent hands.

This book begins there, in the ancestral earth and resilience of my people. It is my tribute to the hands that tilled the land with hope in their hearts, the hearts that held tight through storms that tried to break us, and the spirits that danced when the weight finally lifted. Through these pages, I carry them forward—not just in memory, but in purpose. Because legacy is not only what we inherit—it is what we choose to pass on. And I choose to pass on love, rooted deep in the land where my people prayed and planted.

Follow the Process: A Story of Perseverance, Purpose and Passing the Torch

CHAPTER 1

THE EARLY YEARS OF GWENDOLYN (GWEN) BROWN

My life's journey began on March 29, 1951, during the tense backdrop of the Korean War. I was born to a young, unwed mother, Mary Frances, just 17 years old at the time. The stories passed down to me paint a picture of those early days as marked by hardship and uncertainty.

On the day I was born, my mother's beloved uncle, Harold, was shipped overseas to serve on the front lines. Their relationship was unique—close in age, they had grown up more like siblings than uncle and niece. His departure, paired with the overwhelming responsibilities of new motherhood, must have felt like two great losses for her—one to war, the other to the demands of raising a child alone.

Despite her youth, my mother possessed a clarity that many people never reach in a lifetime. She understood that she couldn't provide the security I needed—emotionally, physically, mentally, financially, or spiritually. In a deeply selfless act of love, she entrusted my upbringing to her Aunt Alice and Uncle Randolph. They accepted the responsibility with open hearts, raising me not out of duty but out of pure, unwavering love—as their own daughter.

As I reflect on my journey from infancy to adulthood, certain moments stand out as foundational to the person I became. So I invite you now to journey with me down Gwen's Memory Lane. Climb aboard with an open heart, leave your judgments at the station, and take in the landscape of a life lived with intention and resilience.

Early Childhood Life

It was early morning, and a brisk cold floated through our little four-room house. I could hear my Daddy rising and preparing for the day ahead. His ritual never changed: he woke early, stirred the glowing coals in the potbelly stove, and warmed the house before Mommy and I got up.

He always made sure the coffee pot was on the stove so Mommy could start her morning with her favorite Red Bag Coffee. That percolating sound and rich aroma were her cue to begin the day.

By then, I would be sitting up in my crib, waiting for Daddy to come scoop me up with his big hugs and kisses on my rosy cheeks. I knew I was his little princess. He would lay out my gray baby blanket on the floor and wrap me up tightly to protect me from the chill outside.

"Baby, come on. It's time to get you ready to stay with your Nana until I get home from work," he'd say. With a small whimper and tearful eyes, I'd plead, "Daddy, don't leave me."

"Baby, I have to go to work," he'd gently reply, hugging me once more. I believed everything Daddy told me. His soft, soothing voice calmed me to the core of my soul.

Then off I would go, crawling toward my baby blanket. Daddy would bundle me up tightly and hold me in his strong arms.

Toddler Age

About two years later, it was one of those bright, beautiful spring mornings when the whole world felt alive and cheerful. The flowers had woken up, their petals stretching wide to show off their pretty colors. The grass was soft and green, tickling the earth like a giant, fluffy rug. Birds sang their morning songs, fluttering from tree to tree, and the air—oh, the air!—smelled as sweet as honeysuckles climbing the fence, as rich as roses blooming outside my window, and as fresh as sunshine mixed with warm dirt after the rain.

Mommy had decided to take a walk across the big, open field to have a cup of coffee with Papa. She thought I'd stay asleep while she was gone—but she was so wrong. My eyes popped open, and the first thing I did was call out, "Mommy! Mommy!" But she didn't answer. I called again, louder this time. Still, nothing.

I sat up, scanning my crib, trying to come up with a plan. How could I get out of this thing? My little hands gripped the railings, and I pulled myself up on wobbly legs. One foot swung up and over, then the other. And just like that—I did it! I was out of my crib!

I marched to the kitchen door, my little feet pattering across the cool floor. The smell of breakfast had faded, but the air outside smelled even better—like Nana's roses, soft and sweet, and the honeysuckle curling thick around the fence, sugary and wild. I pushed open the screen door, and a warm breeze rushed over me, carrying the scent of wildflowers and damp earth.

Now what?

I paused for a second, thinking hard. Then it came to me—Nana and Papa lived across the field. That's where Mommy must have gone. And that's where I needed to be.

I stepped into the tall grass, my tiny toes brushing against the soft blades. The whole field felt alive—bees buzzing in the clover, butterflies flipping and fluttering ahead of me, little bugs hopping leaf to leaf. The honeysuckle smell was even stronger now, thick and magical, blending with the roses that grew wild near Papa's porch. I felt so small—but not scared. Not even a little.

I kept walking, stepping over twigs and tiny hills in the dirt. There might have been wild animals out there—snakes or something scary—but I didn't feel afraid. I just felt brave. I believed that maybe God had sent angels to walk with me, keeping me safe on my big adventure.

And then, finally, I saw Nana and Papa's big house! I hurried up the steps, my little legs climbing as fast as they could. And when I reached the door—there they were: Mommy and Papa!

They looked at me with wide eyes and open mouths. They couldn't believe it. How had I gotten there? How had I made it all that way by myself?

I just stood there, grinning, proud of what I'd done. Papa looked at me for a long second. Then his face softened. He smiled and nodded.

"She's really smart," he said.

And he was right.

Major Shift in My Early Years

I was four years old. Up until then, my life had unfolded quietly, without much excitement or trouble. But around that time, everything began to shift.

My mommy was gravely ill. I was too young to understand what was really happening, but I remember the scene vividly. It was late evening, and she was lying in bed, groaning and moaning in pain. The small bedroom was crowded with her sisters, cousins, and other women I didn't recognize, all gathered around her, praying fervently for healing.

I sat on the sofa in the next room, small and frightened, peering into the bedroom. Fear pressed against my chest, growing heavier with each passing moment. I didn't know what was going on—only that something was terribly wrong. Mommy was sick, and Daddy, my strong and steady Daddy, looked like he was falling apart. His face twisted with desperation, and it frightened me. I'd never seen him like that before.

Someone had called the family doctor—or gone to find her. Dr. Bulaski, a name I'd heard before but had never felt the weight of until that night. I believe she was of Polish descent—a kind woman, a healer who treated everyone with dignity. When she arrived, she moved quickly, examining Mommy, then turned to Daddy and said something that hit like thunder in that quiet house:

"Take her to the hospital. Now."

Suddenly, the room came alive with motion. The women moved with trembling hands, gently helping Mommy get dressed, as if they were afraid she might break. Daddy and Aunt Bert packed me into the car—we weren't leaving me behind. I clung to the seat, too scared to speak. The ride to the hospital passed in a blur—headlights, murmured voices, and the sound of tires against the road.

When we arrived, they took Mommy inside right away. The moment she disappeared behind those hospital doors, it felt like the air left the world.

We waited.

The minutes dragged like years. I must have fallen asleep at some point, though I don't remember closing my eyes. Then suddenly, there were voices—movement—the doctor emerging from the hallway.

"She made it through."

Those words washed over us like rain after a drought. Mommy had survived. But she would stay in the hospital for weeks.

Since Daddy had to work, Aunt Bert took care of me. She rode the bus from Quinton to Richmond every single day, never failing—except for one. That was the day I had misbehaved, and as punishment, she didn't take me to see Mommy. After that, I didn't test her patience again. I made sure to be a good little girl until Mommy came home.

Even though the hospital had strict rules about children visiting, the nurses didn't turn me away. Their eyes were soft, filled with something like love. Maybe they knew I needed to see her. Maybe they saw the ache in my little body.

They let me in.

Their whispers were gentle as they guided me past the big doors. The hospital smelled strange—like medicine and too much bleach—but I didn't care. I was going to see Mommy. My feet hardly made a sound on the cold floor, but my heart pounded with something I didn't have a name for—relief, maybe. Love.

When I finally saw her, I stopped in my tracks. She looked tired. But she was still Mommy. And when she held my hand, even just for a moment, the world made sense again.

After six long weeks, she came home.

Because of her surgery and the uncomfortable straw mattresses, Daddy couldn't sleep beside her. Remember my great crib escape? My parents saw that as a sign: if I was big enough to climb out on my own, I was big enough to have a room of my own. So they decided to add another bedroom to the house.

While Mommy healed, Daddy and I shared the new room. One night, I lay next to him, listening to his steady snoring—soft, rhythmic, almost like music. The house was dark and quiet. I stared at the doorway, wide awake.

And then—I saw something.

A figure. Or maybe it was just my imagination. But it stood in the doorway and slowly walked toward the side of the bed I was on. I froze. And then I screamed. Loud.

Daddy jolted awake and grabbed me.

"What's wrong?" he asked.

Mommy, still in recovery, rushed across the house to reach me. I was sobbing.

"There was someone standing by the bed," I told them.

Daddy, still groggy, muttered,

"That ain't nothing but the devil."

Why he said that, I don't know. Maybe he was tired and didn't know what else to say. Maybe he was trying to protect me from asking too many questions—questions I always had. I was curious by nature. I wanted to understand everything.

But even in moments like that—moments of distance, silence, or confusion—my love for Daddy never wavered. It lived deep inside me, steady and sure. Nothing he said or didn't say could change that.

Launching of My Spiritual Journey

At that pivotal point in my life, around the tender and inquisitive age of five, let's take a little detour and travel down what I like to call Gwen's Spiritual Boulevard.

It was a beautiful Sunday morning. I woke to the comforting sound of Mommy rattling pots and pans—cooking breakfast and preparing for Sunday dinner. The delicious aroma of coffee and sizzling bacon filled the house. The radio was playing gospel music and sermons that etched themselves deep into my heart and soul as we got ready for church. Just to name a few of the great artists and voices that shaped those mornings: The Caravans, The Dixie Hummingbirds, Pilgrim Travelers, Mahalia Jackson, The Soul Stirrers, Rev. James Cleveland, Rev. C. L. Franklin, Albertina Walker, Bishop C.E. Patterson, The Roberta Martin Singers, The Golden Jubilees, and Roberta Thorpe.

When it was time to eat, my Daddy sat at the head of the table, and I sat beside him on his right-hand side in my little chair. Mommy sat at the other end. Daddy always said the blessing over our food:

"Lord, thank you and bless this food that has been prepared for us and for the nourishment of our body and soul. Amen."

Daddy loved all kinds of food, and he was always encouraging me to try something new. He never forced me, but if Daddy offered it, I was going to eat it—no questions asked.

Mommy had laid out my clothes the night before, so all I needed was a little help from Daddy to get dressed. You see, either Mommy or Daddy always gave me a bath on Saturday night, so come Sunday morning, I was clean and ready to go.

My Sunday dress, shoes, and yes—even my panties—were special. They had the days of the week printed on them, so of course, I wore my **"Sunday panties."**

While I got dressed, Mommy put on her church best. And when I say "best," I mean head-to-toe coordinated perfection. Her shoes, hat, walking suit, gloves, and pocketbook all matched in color and style. She looked like she had just stepped out of a fashion magazine—ready to worship in elegance.

Once we were all dressed, we piled into the car to go to church. Wait! Not yet—we had to pick up Sis Alma, my great-grandmother's sister. That's why we called her **"Sis Alma."**

She lived about three-quarters of a mile down a dirt road from our house. Picking her up was a weekly task for Mommy, who took her to every church event she attended. From my little eyes, Sis Alma was just a few inches shy of being a midget. She had bowlegs and waddled to the car like a duck, using her umbrella as a walking stick to keep her balance.

Then we were off to **Union Baptist Church**, established sometime in the early 1860s in rural New Kent County, Virginia.

As we arrived on the church grounds, the Quinton community was out in full force, dressed in their Sunday best for Sunday School and the 11:00 a.m. service. Sunday School was a big deal for us kids—it was where our first real friendships bloomed outside of our immediate families. We couldn't wait to see the friends we hadn't seen since the previous week.

Inside the church, we all got ready for Sunday School. We knew exactly where everyone was going to sit—**no one** dared sit in Miss So-and-So's seat. That had been her seat since the beginning of time, and she wasn't about to give it up for anybody.

Sunday School began with Deacon Lanza Minor, the Sunday School Superintendent, offering a heartfelt welcome and prayer. Then Mrs. Martha West, our church pianist, led the congregational hymn,

"What a Friend We Have in Jesus."

Afterward, we split into our Sunday School classes. Union Baptist only had one large sanctuary, so classes were held in each corner of the church:

- **Beginner's Class (ages 2–5):** taught by Mrs. Martha West
- **Intermediate Class (ages 6–12):** taught by Mrs. Alma Lightfoot
- **Junior Class (ages 13–18):** taught by Mrs. Mary Lou Williams
- **Adult Class (ages 19+):** taught by Deacon William Christian

It was hard to concentrate with all the activity in that one big room, but somehow, we managed to tune out the distractions and focus on our lesson. Sunday School mattered to me. I was learning about the Bible's great characters and the roles they played in building the Kingdom of God.

CHAPTER 2

THE ROOTS OF MY ANCESTRIAL VILLAGE LEGACY

The Christian-Carter-Brown Ancestral Village

Now, after our brief detour down my Spiritual Boulevard—and before I continue my personal journey—allow me to share a few things about the Christian–Carter–Brown Ancestral Village: a place where the roots of our family run deep, woven with both hardship and unyielding resilience.

My great-grandparents, Nana and Papa—Ida Carter Christian and William Albert Christian—were the children of people born into slavery during the 1850s. A slave owner named Jane E. Carter raised them on a plot of land she owned. According to the New Kent County deed books, this sacred ground was located in the Bottoms Bridge area, between Route 60 and old Route 33 (today's Route 249). It was part of more than 300 acres known as "The Island." But this land was more than soil and trees—our ancestors toiled, loved, suffered, and dreamed here, forging their spirits under the heavy yoke of bondage.

When emancipation came in 1865, it rippled through our community with life-altering force. Freedom brought with it the possibility of something previously unimaginable: ownership. In that historic moment, several formerly enslaved people were able to purchase parcels of land from Ms. Carter. Among them were Nana and Papa's parents—specifically, Isham Carter and his wife Alice Friend Carter, and Harrison Christian and his wife Octavia Ellyson Christian. They acquired their own pieces of "The Island." Other families, including the descendants of John and Thomas Brown—who had labored on these lands for generations—also secured homesteads once they gained their freedom.

For nearly seventy years, as generations came and went, that land thrived as a working farm and as the heartbeat of a self-sufficient community. Everything one needed to eat came straight from the earth. The fields yielded a bounty: corn, watermelons, cantaloupes, green beans, butter beans, cucumbers, squash, and both sweet and white potatoes. Tomatoes, eggplants, and green and red bell peppers grew in abundance, alongside kale, mustard greens, turnips, and collard greens.

And it didn't stop at produce. Our people raised rabbits, pigs, chickens, cows, ducks, geese, goats, horses, and mules—a bustling and diverse menagerie that kept the entire village nourished and whole.

At the heart of this rich tapestry were the women of the Christian, Carter, and Brown families—keepers of tradition, nurturers of spirit, and givers of life. Their legacy is one of love, labor, and community, passed down through every shared meal, every quilt stitched by hand, every hand that tilled the land, and every soul that walked it with purpose.

This, then, is the Christian–Carter–Brown Ancestral Village—a living testament to survival, unity, and the profound courage of our forebears. A legacy defined not only by hardship but also by the joy of shared abundance, the dignity of work, and the deep bonds that continue to sustain our family today.

Our village breathed with the rhythm of interconnected lives. Down every dirt road, around every bend, lived the people who shaped my understanding of love, resilience, and the transformative power of standing together.

Ida and William Albert Christian Home Estate

Nana and Papa's house sat just off the main highway, nestled amid acres of open farmland. Oh my God—pulling into their yard was like stepping into a dream. The beauty of the landscape was breathtaking. Their big, beautiful, nine-room, two-story white house stood tall and proud, surrounded by vibrant life. The scent of mint bushes under the kitchen window was crisp and refreshing. Snowball bushes, mimosa trees, blooming tulips, lavender, fruit trees—everywhere you looked, nature showed off her splendor. It was simply mind-blowing.

Our journey through generations didn't begin in the fields but inside that house—where our elders nurtured faith and whispered legacy into our hearts. That home held more than walls and rooms; it held our beginnings.

We climbed the steps and entered the kitchen, where our eyes were drawn to the old cooking stove, its warmer perched on top like a familiar centerpiece. Near the dining room door stood the icebox, its only job to keep food cool with a single block of ice. Of course, curiosity took over—we had to open it. Inside were just a few things: a block of cheese, some homemade butter from Mama's churning, and bottles of fresh milk from our cow, Sally.

We continued our walk through time.

In the kitchen cupboard, rows upon rows of mason jars gleamed—each one sealed tightly, holding summer's bounty in waiting. We moved into the heart of the home: the dining room. It wasn't just a place to eat—it was where family warmth and the rich smells of home-cooked meals wrapped themselves around us.

Beside the wall stood the big wood-burning stove, always warm, always ready to heat a kettle or warm a biscuit. Firewood had already been chopped and stacked neatly in the wooden box beside the door. Harriet—though everyone called her Sis—sat on the worn sofa near the stove, shelling butter beans or peas, her soft humming blending with the gentle creaks of the old house.

We stepped down the hallway that connected the main rooms of the home. The floorboards creaked with familiarity. In the middle of the hall sat the old glider, where Nana and Papa would often sit in silence, soaking in the hush of summer evenings while a soft breeze floated through the screen doors.

Across the hallway was the mysterious living room—off-limits to us kids. It was reserved for special occasions and even more special guests. The room seemed preserved, like a museum of memories. A Kimble Player piano stood proud near the far wall, silent but full of history. On the coffee table rested the family Bible, its worn leather cover catching the afternoon light. Nana always told us, "My son Harold sent this to me when he was in the Army," her voice filled with pride. He had sent it from Korea.

Nana and Papa's bedroom was across the hall from the living room. The bed sat near the window, and a wood stove warmed the opposite side. Nana spent most of her time there due to her declining health. She struggled with high blood pressure and heart issues, and cataracts had dimmed her sight. She was partially blind. When Papa wasn't in the fields plowing, he would sit in the room beside her, reading the newspaper or watching "The Ed Sullivan Show" and "The Ted Mack Show" on a small black-and-white TV gifted to him by his daughter Ruth.

There wasn't much else to see on the first floor, so we headed upstairs.

The stairway was tucked in the dining room. At the top of the stairs, to the left, was the bedroom of Nana and Papa's youngest daughter, Virginia Octavia—whom everyone lovingly called Tweedie Weedie. She lived there with her partner, James, and their three children: Debra, Sandra (aka Man), and Anthony (aka Chubby). In the corner of the room stood a cupboard James had built himself, carefully stocked with canned food and personal belongings.

Just across the hall was my cousin Joan's room. Toward the back of the house were three more bedrooms. The one on the left belonged to my cousin Helen. In the middle room, my cousins Larry, Vann, and Bennie (short for Benjamin) shared a lively, boy-filled space. The far-right bedroom belonged to my Aunt Sis, one of Nana and Papa's younger children. She had a twin brother named Harold. Though Sis had a crippled leg, she carried herself with quiet strength and grace.

As we exited the "big house," we stood in the backyard, soaking in the peaceful yet energizing spirit of the Christian Home Estate. The yard had no grass—we were responsible for sweeping it with straw brooms handmade by Nana. Though only four to six years old at the time, we had our chores and completed them joyfully, often turning it into a game to see who could sweep the most.

At the far end of the yard stood a great shade tree where we often escaped the blazing sun. Across from it grew a plum tree, loaded with big, juicy plums we'd snack on while playing.

Near the burning bush stood the birdhouse Nana had built just for the martins. Each spring, those glossy little birds migrated north and returned to Nana's yard, year after year. She always said they were a blessing—they ate the bugs that threatened the crops.

Looking across the road from the house, just past the clothesline, stood a tall pear tree bearing what folks swore were the juiciest pears in all of New Kent County. A little farther down that dirt road was the apple and peach orchard. And beyond that, a towering wild cherry tree stood proud. My cousins—Jackie, Mousie, Bennie, Vann—and I, along with neighborhood kids, spent countless hours under that cherry tree, building sandcastles in the road until Papa's nephew-in-law, Judge Minor, came barreling through and ruined our hard work.

When it came to food, Nana and Papa grew or raised nearly everything you could imagine. Corn, watermelons, cantaloupes, green beans, butter beans, cucumbers, squash, tomatoes—you name it, they had it. During harvest time, our whole family and neighbors came together to gather the crops. Nana and my Mommy would can the vegetables and make preserves from the fruits. There was always enough to share. No one in our village ever went hungry.

Eventually, we wandered over to the barn, where the animals were kept and roamed freely. The large two-story barn housed our horses, Nellie and Prince. Nellie was deep brown, nearly black, and Prince was a handsome light brown stallion. They were strong, hardworking animals who helped plow the fields and pull the wagon during harvest. The hay was stored in the loft, and the corn bins sat on the ground floor.

But the barn wasn't just for animals—it was a playground for us cousins. We'd climb the ladder and play in the hayloft for hours. Just beside the barn stood a magnificent weeping willow. Its graceful branches offered beauty and comfort, a perfect gathering place.

Every Sunday, my cousin Larry's father, Elijah Green, would drive down from Richmond to spend time with him. They would sit for hours under that weeping willow beside the barn. Few words were exchanged, but the bond between them was unmistakable and profound—something beyond explanation.

Nana and Papa's farm always reminded me of that old song:
"Old MacDonald had a farm—E-I-E-I-O."

Martha and Dave Armstead Lane

After leaving Nana and Papa's Home Estate, we walked down the old dirt road, venturing into the heart of the Village—a realm where their legacy lived on through daughters, grandchildren, nieces, nephews, and cousins. The soft hum of nature accompanied our steps as the early morning light revealed flowers budding with quiet hope, trees swaying in a gentle dance, vegetables pushing eagerly through the rich soil, and birds soaring overhead. All around us, the chorus of insects and frogs created a majestic symphony, setting the tone for our journey.

We arrived at Aunt Martha's little red four-room house, perched high on a hill where dull moments had no place. In their place thrived the vibrant pulse of life and unyielding resilience. As the third-born of Nana and Papa, Aunt Martha carried the formidable responsibility of raising six children—William (Bill), Erselle, Ida, Alice (affectionately called Shortie), Mildred (Millie), and Jacqueline (Jackie). Life in her home was a tapestry of quiet strength, woven from steadfast routine and tender care.

Before dawn broke, Aunt Martha would already be at work—baking hot biscuits, crisping savory fatback, and stirring a hearty pot of oatmeal. These morning rituals were her way of nourishing and grounding her children before they faced the day. Then, with a heart full of both hope and sorrow, she'd head to the highway to catch a ride to Richmond, where she labored as a cook and restaurant worker. Behind her steady rhythm of sacrifice were silent tears, glistening beneath the surface—the weight of Bro. Dave's mental health struggles casting long shadows over their lives.

As Aunt Martha's children grew into their teenage years, the house transformed. After the morning chores were done, the home filled with the laughter and spirited chatter of neighborhood youth. Teenagers crowded into corners, sneaking cigarettes and gathering around tables for rounds of Bid Whist and Spades, waiting for their parents to return from long days cleaning houses, cooking in restaurants, or working in factories. Meanwhile, we young'uns roamed the woods, played tag ball and hide-and-seek, or chased June bugs, tying strings to their legs for our mischievous amusement. In those carefree hours, we felt the freedom of childhood wrapped in the safety of the community.

Just across the field stood my Mommy and Daddy's home—a sanctuary of love, a steady counterpoint to the struggles only a few yards away. During difficult episodes when Bro. Dave's troubles escalated, Aunt Martha would summon the strength to carry her youngest daughter, Jackie, across that familiar stretch of earth to our home. It was a quiet act of desperation and love, rooted in trust and maternal protection. From the very beginning, my parents filled in the gaps when they could—dressing Bill when he was still a toddler, helping ease burdens too heavy for Aunt Martha to carry alone.

When Ida, the third oldest, came to live with us at around eleven or twelve, she became both helper and protector. Her quiet presence was a gift—bringing stability and affection to our home, and strengthening the deep bonds between our families.

That winding path we traveled—known as Armstead Lane—was etched with memory. Every crack in the road, every whisper of wind through the trees carried the stories of family, endurance, and the fierce love that bound us together. In that stretch of land, among the blooms and rustling branches, Nana and Papa's legacy grew strong—a living narrative of hope, sacrifice, and the quiet joy of simply being together.

Armstead Lane was more than a road. It was a passage through the soul of our familial history. It bore the tenderness of Aunt Martha's resilience, the mischief and laughter of youth, and the protective embrace of home. With each step, we walked in the footprints of those who had come before us—honoring a legacy that still nourishes our soul.

Little Pioneers: Rediscovering Our Ancestral Village

Morning sunlight spilled across the horizon as we finished our chores, eager to embrace the freedom of the day. The village was our playground—vast, boundless, and full of promise. It stretched beyond what our young minds could fathom, a realm shaped by the survival instincts and quiet wisdom passed down through generations. There were no clocks, no structured schedules—only the rhythm of nature guiding us, teaching us, molding us.

To the left, nestled deep within the forest, our secret gathering place awaited. The dense woods, under our touch, transformed into an enchanted kingdom where imagination reigned supreme. Vann and I slipped naturally into our familiar roles as "mommy and daddy," guiding our make-believe village of Jackie, Mousie, Pinkie, Bennie, and the rest of our cousins. We built homes from sticks and dreams, weaving stories stitched with the kind of joy only childhood could bring.

Hunger didn't send us running home—instead, the land provided. Wild blueberries and blackberries lined the roadside, ripe and waiting to be plucked. We feasted on nature's bounty, our fingers stained deep with the hues of summer's harvest. To the right, Mr. Minor's cornfield stretched wide, and beneath its towering stalks, walnut and persimmon trees stood like ancient guardians of our childhood. With rocks in hand, we cracked open walnuts, their earthy richness mingling with the sweet tang of persimmons—a meal not made in kitchens, but crafted by young explorers who trusted the land's generosity.

Time was not measured by ticking hands or ringing bells. It was carved into the sky. Our elders had taught us to read the sun, and when it stood directly overhead, we knew—it was noon. Stomachs rumbled in agreement, our bodies recognizing the language of the day, nudging us homeward.

That village—our sacred ground—held our childhood like a treasured storybook. Every path, every tree, every whisper of wind carried the echoes of who we were: little pioneers, navigating the world with bare feet, hungry hearts, and an untamed spirit.

Ella and Judge Minor Lane

Not far from Aunt Martha and Bro. Dave's home lived Cousin Ella. Ella and Judge Minor Lane added a layer of complexity to our understanding of family dynamics. Cousin Ella, Papa's niece, had married Judge Minor, and together they brought ten children into the world. But something in the air around their house felt heavy—suffocating—like an unspoken grief woven into the very walls.

Mr. Minor commanded fear more than respect. His presence drained the light from a room. Everyone knew the truth that lay behind closed doors—Judge Minor was cruel, emotionally, mentally, and physically abusive. His shadow loomed large, and his cruelty left silent scars that many carried without words.

Then, one fall day, tragedy struck. While the Village worked and the children sat in school, flames consumed their home. When the sun set, the Minor household was no more. Everything was lost.

Without hesitation, Mommy and Daddy's house became theirs too—a sanctuary for the displaced, a safe place to rebuild fractured lives. Despite the darkness Mr. Minor brought with him, our home remained a refuge. It was a place where faith held steady and love softened the sharp edges of suffering.

After six months, the Minor family returned to their land and began rebuilding from the ground up. The fire had taken much, but not their spirit. They rose again, not unbroken, but unbowed.

And while they moved forward, the imprint of those months remained—a quiet reminder that even fractured families can find shelter in the storm. That love makes room. That healing, though often slow and uncertain, sometimes begins around a shared table.

With the Minor family gone and the house once again our own, a different kind of silence settled in—one that would soon give way to new beginnings, new challenges, and lessons I had not yet imagined.

A Legacy Woven in Time

The gravel crunched softly beneath our feet as we walked down that familiar road, the wind carrying whispers of those who had come before. Just a quarter mile from Minor Lane, we arrived at the home of Cousin Rebecca—affectionately known as Cousin Beck—and her husband, Ollie Moss.

Cousin Beck's roots ran close to mine. She was the daughter of Arthur and Mamie Christian. Mamie, the sister of my great-grandmother Nana, was deeply etched into our family's story—a quiet matriarch whose spirit lingered in our traditions, her presence felt in the gentle echoes of family rituals and shared meals.

Before we even stepped onto their homeplace, I felt the pull of history. It was more than just a home—it was the **Harrison and Octavia (Tavee) Christian Homestead Place**. Grandpa Harrison and Grandma Tavee had built that house with their own hands and hearts, raising four children within its walls: James (Jim), Lottie Ann, Cora, and my great-grandfather, William Albert.

After their passing, the eldest son, Uncle Jim, carried on the legacy with his wife, Lula Cross. Together, they raised eight children in that same home, filling the space with laughter, struggle, renewal, and the rhythms of everyday life.

Time moved Uncle Jim and Aunt Lula's children onward. They grew, scattered, and forged new paths. But the homestead remained—steadfast, patient, waiting for the next caretakers of memory.

When Cousin Beck and Cousin Ollie married, they returned to that very soil, anchoring themselves in the ground of our shared past. As we approached their porch, I paused—remembering the hands that had shaped this space, the stories echoing in its rafters like an old song.

And there we were again—standing where another thread had been woven into the family's tapestry. Cousin Beck and Cousin Ollie lived the legacy now, adding their chapter to the land that had held us for so long.

Moss Agape Love Cove

Cousin Beck and Cousin Ollie's home had always been more than just a house—it was a soft place to land, a living testament to what love looked like when it was rooted deep. From the moment your foot touched the porch, you were met with an unspoken welcome, the kind of quiet hospitality that didn't need to be announced—it simply existed. You felt it in the air, in the laughter drifting from the kitchen, in the way the chairs never seemed to mind who was sitting in them.

At the heart of that haven was Cousin Beck's sacred space—her kitchen. It was a place where flavors spoke history and every dish told a story. You could practically hear the sizzle of cornbread batter meeting hot cast iron, smell the rich perfume of slow-cooked greens, and feel the generations stirring in every pot. She cooked like she was praying—with intention, with love, and with reverence for where she came from. Beck's meals didn't just fill you up—they brought you home.

Just outside, Cousin Ollie tended to a garden that was part miracle, part memory. His hands, shaped by years of honest work and quiet care, pulled life from the ground like a hymn. Every row, every bloom, bore his patience, his steadiness, his unspoken joy. Together, they cultivated more than food—they cultivated connection, comfort, and the kind of stillness that made a person want to stay a while.

Their legacy carried forward in their children, George and Delores—each one a living branch of that rooted love.

Delores, gentle and graceful, was her mother's shadow in the kitchen and her own light in the community. She moved through the house like a blessing, absorbing every lesson Cousin Beck offered—not just in recipes, but in the quiet art of nurturing. From kneading dough to cradling conversation, Delores carried the tradition forward, binding past and future with love as her thread. What she offered wasn't just food—it was welcome. It was presence. It was legacy in motion.

George, meanwhile, sang with a voice dipped in soul and centuries. There was something ancestral in it, something that held grief and glory in the same breath. Inspired by gospel giants like Sam Cooke, George didn't just perform—he ministered. Backed by his quartet brothers—Bill Armstead, Floyd, Andrew and Ralph Morris, and John Crump—their harmony became more than music. It was balm. It was faith turned into melody.

Each time they sang—whether from a church pew or beneath an open sky—their voices wrapped around the community like a prayer. George's gift, steeped in heritage and shaped by heartache and hope, became a bridge between generations. A reminder that even in sorrow, there is song.

That was the **Moss Agape Love Cove**. A place where love was baked into bread, sung into being, and passed down in gestures too subtle to name. A place where time slowed down and the soul exhaled. It wasn't just a home—it was a living story of who we were when we chose love, again and again

The Alma and John Lightfoot Cul-de-sac

Just down the road from Cousin Beck and Cousin Ollie's stood the home of Sis Alma and Cousin John—a cherished dwelling rooted in generations of family history. Sis Alma, my great-grandmother Nana's half-sister, was born to Isham Carter's second wife, tying her firmly into the fabric of our legacy. She and Cousin John lived on land Isham acquired after emancipation—a quiet but powerful testament to resilience, endurance, and hope.

Their roots reached deep. Cousin John, son of Papa's sister Cora and Louis Lightfoot, brought together the lines of both Nana and Papa. Together, he and Sis Alma raised their bright granddaughter Jean in a home steeped in faith, love, and steady wisdom.

Though small in stature, Sis Alma carried a mighty spirit. Her home radiated care, and her presence filled every room with a kind of quiet strength. One of my favorite memories was fetching water from their spring, greeted on the way back uphill by the smell—and taste—of her hot rolls. Those moments were more than chores; they were lessons in joy, reward, and the generous language of love.

When Cousin John began to struggle with the lingering effects of his World War I service, Mommy would send me and my sister to assist Sis Alma. In those moments, we witnessed the calm power of Sis Alma's daily rhythm—always beginning with prayer, grounding the home in faith and grace before the day had even begun.

Cousin John was a quiet anchor. A man of few words, he taught by example—building fences, sharing meals, working the sawmill. His presence uplifted all who knew him. Porch evenings were marked by his humble humor and stories that made us laugh long after the sun had set. He came to Christ later in life and became a devoted Deacon at

Union Baptist Church, anchoring his faith as firmly as he had anchored his family.

Their legacy lived in every hot roll baked and every quiet lesson shared.

Jean, the daughter of their firstborn, Mary, lived with them during the school year. She wasn't just a granddaughter—she was a living symbol of all they stood for. Curious and kind, Jean soaked in the wisdom around her—through books, through kitchen chores, through long evenings listening to Cousin John's gentle stories. Creativity bloomed in her. She drew, she wrote, she made things with her hands and heart, nurtured daily by the love and patience that surrounded her.

Jean's presence wasn't just joyful—it was generational. In her, the lessons of resilience, faith, and devotion took root and blossomed. She was the promise that everything planted in the past could still flourish in the future. Through her, the spirit of our family legacy lived on—nurtured, strengthened, and ready to grow again.

The Alberta and Ernest Crump Loveland Haven Road

The Alberta and Ernest Crump Loveland Haven Road brought to life the old nursery rhyme about the "old lady who lived in a shoe" with so many children she didn't know what to do.

From the moment you arrived, cousins spilled into the yard like sunlight—laughter echoing across the modest but vibrant Crump household. With sixteen children—some grown and gone, others still filling the halls with youthful energy—life pulsed through every corner. Cousin Alberta and Mr. Ernest's love anchored it all.

Their home etched itself into our memories, not simply as a house, but as a sanctuary. It was a place where laughter echoed, grief found comfort, and belonging was as natural as breathing. Love lived in every wall, every warm meal, every embrace at the door.

Though sorrow visited with the heartbreaking loss of three beloved children—Ruby, Arthur, and Alex—it didn't splinter the family; it drew the Christian-Carter-Brown Village even closer. Grief became a thread that stitched us together more tightly, bound by shared memory, prayer, and grace.

Yet through it all, Cousin Alberta's kindness never faded. Her heart made room for everyone. Neighborhood children found more than playmates—they found home. Her kitchen was a place of quiet magic, where homemade walnut pound cake appeared like a sacrament, and where you were seen, heard, and loved.

The yard, the porch, the riverbank—they became classrooms. Under the gentle guidance of Cousin Alberta, her sister Beck, and cousins Louberta and Idabell, we learned to live with presence. We picked berries, baked rolls, cleaned fish, and soaked up the wisdom passed down through gestures and glances more than words.

Those fishing trips to Bottoms Bridge left a permanent mark. The women fashioned poles from pliable branches, tying lines and hooks with fingers that moved like they remembered something older than themselves. Along the Chickahominy River, we waited—sometimes for fish, always for wonder.

Cousin Alberta, regal in her practicality and poise, remained at home to nurture the heart of the family while Mr. Ernest worked hard to provide. She affectionately called him "Daddy"—a title rich with tenderness and earned respect. Their marriage was quiet but powerful, built not on display but on devotion. Though gentle and sweet, she ruled her home with grace and firm love—undisputed queen of her castle.

Their home wasn't just another stop on a dusty back road—it was a refuge. Its "welcome hinges" never rusted. Whether guests came with joy or burden, they left with hearts a little fuller, spirits a little lighter. Cousin Alberta and Mr. Ernest modeled a love that was both ordinary and heroic—a love expressed not in grand gestures but in the sacred rhythm of daily care.

Their legacy lives on—not only in stories or photographs but in the scent of walnut cake, the echo of river songs, the soft memory of hands that held firm and hearts that stayed wide open. They showed us that the truest homes are built with more than wood and nails—they're built with open doors, listening ears, and love that endures

Gussie Brown and Lucy Christian (GBLC) Estate

The dirt road stretched before us like a well-worn invitation, promising adventure and the boundless freedom of childhood. We were village kids—barefoot, bright-eyed, and bold—laughing and chattering as we kicked up little clouds of dust, leaving Nana and Papa's house behind.

That familiar pear tree leaned into the curve of the road, its golden fruit hanging low, daring us to pluck it mid-run. Blackberry bushes lined the edges like thorny sentinels, guarding their treasure with sharp little warnings, offering sweet rewards to those brave—or reckless—enough to reach in.

A little farther along, the cornfield rose up like a green cathedral—its tall stalks forming a leafy fortress around us. We darted through its maze of whispering rows, hidden from the world, swallowed by the joy of play. Every rustle felt like part of the game. That freedom—it felt infinite.

Then came the soft welcome of Mrs. Gussie Brown's home, nestled in the calm of that sacred stretch of land. Her son Alton—lovingly called Bony Jaw—and her mother, Miss Lucy, lived there too. Miss Lucy, slight and stooped beneath her bonnet, moved with a grace that came from another time. Even as a child, I could feel her quiet power.

She raised wild rabbits—skittish, soft creatures that seemed plucked from the woods and tamed by her presence. She let me feed them scraps, my small hands trembling with wonder. One day, she placed a rabbit in those hands and said, "Take it." My daddy built it a little house, careful and proud. That rabbit was more than a pet—it was a living gift, a memory wrapped in fur and kindness.

Sometimes I brought her my big questions. "Miss Lucy, what makes you live so long?" I asked, full of childhood awe.

Her answer came without pause: "Nobody but God, baby."

Those words rooted themselves in me like scripture—simple, steady, eternal.

Those walks down the road weren't just part of our day—they were part of who we were. They were the rhythm of our freedom, the shape of our joy. The GBLC Estate wasn't just a place. It pulsed with quiet stories, with legacy, with love that lived in rabbit hutches and blackberries and weathered hands. It carved its name into my memory—not with grandeur, but with grace.

Annie and Garfield Hewlett (AGH) Residence Place

Just across the road from the home of Miss Gussie and Miss Lucy stood the house of Cousin Annie Brown Hewlett and Mr. Garfield Hewlett—a dwelling steeped in resilience, layered with both joy and sorrow. The very walls seemed to breathe history.

Born to Jim and Lula Christian, Cousin Annie—Papa's beloved niece—first married Bennie (Benjamin) Brown, the son of Gussie and Thomas.

Together, they raised seven children: Annie May, Viola (known lovingly as Wiggie), Helen, Gladys, Herman, Jimmy (James), and Edna. But tragedy struck swiftly and cruelly—Bennie died in a Richmond streetcar accident, leaving Cousin Annie to carry the weight of his absence and raise their children alone.

In time, healing arrived in the form of Garfield Hewlett, a skilled carpenter whose hands shaped wood as surely as Cousin Annie shaped home and heart. They married and built a life together, raising four more sons—Russell, Earl, Bobby, and Guy. I was just three years old when I first witnessed Mr. Garfield's quiet magic. He crafted an extra room onto our house with the kind of ease that made wood seem to bend to his will. That room later became sacred to me, the place where I was visited by a guardian angel after Mama returned from the hospital.

But beneath the warmth of that home, heartache lingered.

Wiggie passed away young, leaving behind a husband, Howard Lightfoot, and their infant son, Wayne. Herman succumbed to scleroderma in his thirties. Jimmy survived a harrowing car accident at just sixteen, bearing its mark in a lifelong scar. Lupus cast its shadow across the family line, haunting children and grandchildren alike.

The next generation carried its own share of burden. Russell died in a tragic car crash. Earl, facing learning challenges, left school early and found his own path. Bobby—brilliant, tender-hearted—struggled with addiction and later, HIV/AIDS, which claimed him too soon.

And still, through it all, Cousin Annie's faith never wavered.

Every Sunday, without fail, she took her seat in the second row at Union Baptist Church, surrounded by her circle of praying sisters. Their voices, rising in worship, held her steady. In the face of relentless pain, she found quiet strength—anchored in prayer, community, and her unwavering belief in God.

The Hewlett home was never just a house. It was a sacred vessel of memory, built from grief and grace, sorrow and song, loss and love. Even now, I feel its echoes—soft and strong—as if the house itself is still whispering the stories it held so dearly.

Annabelle Morris and Martha Christian: Dwelling Place of Generations

Just across the road from Cousin Annie and Mr. Garfield's home, no farther than a football field's length, stood the modest four-room house of Ms. Annabelle Morris on Orapax Road. Unassuming in stature but mighty in spirit, it pulsed with the rhythm of multigenerational life—a humble dwelling layered with history, heart, and the ever-evolving story of a family deeply rooted in love.

Inside, every room carried its own rhythm, each space warmed by the presence of voices and footsteps that spanned generations. Ms. Annabelle Morris's children—Andrew, Ralph, Phyllis, Ann, David, and Daniel—moved through the house with ease, their laughter and conversation weaving a symphony of everyday life. In one corner, her older daughters, Phyllis and Grace, lived alongside their own children, adding yet another thread to the tapestry of shared memory. The house hummed with life—babies crying, mothers cooking, children playing, elders remembering.

Adding to that melody was the dignified presence of Ms. Martha Christian—Ms. Annabelle Morris's mother and the matriarchal anchor of the household. Before moving into a cozy three-room house just behind the main home, she shared the space, her quiet strength and steady wisdom guiding the family's daily rhythm. Her move marked the gentle turning of a chapter, just as Grace and her children later moved to Norfolk, Virginia, joining her husband's family—a bittersweet passage in the ongoing dance of change.

The story of that home didn't end with departures. It grew.

When Andrew married Phyllis Minor, space became tight, but love knew how to make room. A trailer was added to the property, and their children joined the ever-expanding household. And still, the little house adapted. It breathed. It stretched. It made space for both the echoes of the past and the footsteps of the future.

Every creak of the floorboards, every curtain fluttering in the afternoon light, whispered of resilience and belonging. The home stood not only as shelter but as witness—to sorrow and celebration, to births and goodbyes, to the sacred ordinary that defined village life.

Standing before it, or sitting within its walls, you could feel something holy—a current of continuity, a legacy etched into the grain of the wood and the soil beneath. It wasn't just a house. It was a living archive, a container of memories and meaning, where each generation added its verse to the song.

Mamie and Arthur Christian Villa

Mamie and Arthur Christian's home was the final, and most fitting, stop on our journey through the Village. Just across the field from the homes of Martha Christian and Annabelle Morris, their house radiated warmth and the quiet strength of deep family bonds. Aunt Mamie moved through her days with gentle grace, even as her health declined. Nana, ever the protective big sister, loved her with a fierce and unwavering devotion—a bond that had held strong since their childhood.

I cherished our joyful walks up the path to Aunt Mamie's house, hand in hand with Nana and my cousins. Each visit shimmered with anticipation and laughter. Outside, we played for hours with cousins Barbara and Emma—the spirited, vibrant daughters of Julia Shelton, Aunt Mamie's youngest. Nearby, Edward, Julia's son, immersed himself in books, sharing comic books and quiet camaraderie with my cousin Larry, two kindred spirits bound by a love of story.

Aunt Mamie's home was more than shelter; it was a sanctuary of memory, laughter, and kinship. Each room held echoes of joy, and every wall bore the soft imprint of legacy. It stood as a reflection of the Village itself—layered, enduring, alive.

Leaving their home, I felt the heartbeat of the Village more deeply than ever. Every family held its own rhythm and song, yet together they formed a resilient, interwoven tapestry of connection and care. The Village wasn't just a place—it was a living history, passed from hand to hand, preserved in tradition, held fast by faith.

Even now, I hear the laughter of children racing through open fields. I remember the games, the stories, and the sacred hush that fell when elders shared their wisdom. The smells of simmering meals, the cadence of work, and the rhythm of voices rising in prayer still linger in my heart.

Those moments taught me the true meaning of unity, devotion, and generational love. Their lessons remain—steady, luminous, and alive within me.

Returning to Nana and Papa's Home

Returning to Nana and Papa's home felt like stepping into the heart of a village square—where open doors signaled open hearts. Over the years, it became more than just a house; it was a foundation, a sanctuary, a place where healing and belonging took root. Alongside Aunt Tweedie Weedie and her family, Nana and Papa's door always swung wide for those in need of a place to land.

My birth mother, Mary Frances—daughter of Coriene; Joan and Helen—daughters of Aunt Bert; Larry—Aunt Idabelle's eldest; Vann and Mousie—the son and daughter of Aunt Lois; and Bennie—Uncle Harold's son—all found shelter and steadfast love under their roof. At the center of it all was Aunt Sis, the eighth-born and Uncle Harold's twin, who never left home—a quiet sentinel in the rhythm of our family's life.

Their hospitality extended beyond kin. I still remembered Ms. Carrie, a dear family friend, who lived with them for a time. And I'd never forget when Aunt Idabelle returned during a difficult season, bringing Mr. Bob and their youngest son, Al. There was always room. The house didn't shrink—it expanded with need, with grace, with love.

It was Nana who anchored the spiritual soul of that home. Her whispered prayer—*"Lord, take care of my children for generations to come"*—still echoed through my memory. As our caregiver while our parents worked, she wrapped her grandchildren and great-grandchildren in the soft folds of her arms and her unwavering faith. I could still see her: our gentle shepherd, leading us little ducklings down the road to visit her sister Mamie. That image remained etched in my soul—a living testament to her quiet strength and enduring devotion.

We didn't just remember Nana's legacy—we *lived* it. In every prayer, every act of kindness, every life she touched with unconditional love, her light endured. She was the heartbeat of our family, and that light still warmed the home that called us back time and again.

Papa, too, stood like a pillar—strong, disciplined, and quietly profound. His love was shaped by an era when duty often stood in for affection, but it ran deep, silent and sure, beneath his stern exterior.

Beyond the boundaries of our home, he was deeply respected—a man of conviction and courage. Alongside my Mommy, he traveled rural roads, urging Black citizens to exercise their right to vote in the wake of the 1964 Voting Rights Act. He served as Chairman of the Deacon Board at Union Baptist—a man of deep faith, quiet scholarship, and unwavering commitment to justice.

And yet, it was through music that Papa revealed his most tender self. His solos, rich with emotion, offered a rare glimpse into feelings he seldom voiced aloud. Songs like *If I Could Hear My Mother Pray Again* and *May the Work I Have Done Speak for Me* filled the sanctuary—and lingered in the hearts of all who heard them.

His legacy lived on—in the principles he stood by, the lives he lifted, and the quiet, steadfast love he expressed through action. Just like the home he and Nana built, Papa reminded us that true belonging isn't found in walls or possessions, but in the hearts that choose to gather—again and again.

CHAPTER 3

Alice and Randolph Brown – Safe Haven Sanctuary Covered in Favor: The Home God Prepared for Me

After leaving Nana and Papa's home, the time had come to return to where *my* story truly begins—the place I call the *Safe Haven Sanctuary*.

We didn't just remember Nana's legacy—we lived it.

With every step I've taken in life, one truth becomes more and more undeniable: **God's favor has covered me since the moment I was conceived**. Let me tell you about Alice and Randolph Brown—my adoptive parents, my protectors, my heart's foundation—who, by Allah's grace and mercy, became the guardians of my soul.

Alice, the second-born child of Nana and Papa, married Randolph Brown on July 12, 1938, in a sacred ceremony at Union Baptist Church in Quinton, Virginia. Rev. Howard Wallace officiated the vows that would bind them in a union rooted in faith, love, and steadfast resilience.

Their first home, nestled across the field from Nana and Papa's homestead on land belonging to the estate of Thomas Brown, brimmed with promise. But tragedy struck when Daddy's brother, Temple, in a drunken stupor, accidentally set the house ablaze. The fire consumed everything they owned.

In the aftermath, Nana and Papa stepped forward with an extraordinary gift: they deeded two acres of adjoining land to Mommy and Daddy. With this blessing and tireless determination, they built a charming Cape Cod-style home with vibrant red siding. More than a structure, it became a refuge—a place of warmth, healing, and hope.

The front yard welcomed visitors with a cascade of colors from Mommy's flower garden, each bloom tended with care and intention. We kept the grass trimmed with a roller mower—a task of pride, not chore.

Behind the house, a generous garden flourished: cucumbers, tomatoes, watermelons, cantaloupes, white and sweet potatoes, sweet corn, and peanuts grew in abundance. It was a feast for the eyes, the soul, and a reminder of our self-sufficiency and joyful labor.

Our animals completed the symphony of life. Chickens, roosters, and guinea hens clucked and cooed; rabbits hopped about; and our spirited horse, Nellie, held a special place in all our hearts. Even the pigs had their place in the harmony. At the center of the yard stood an old well, from which we drew water—each bucket a connection to the land and its blessings.

Inside, our home was a sanctuary of love and creativity. Mommy's hand was evident in every corner—doilies, crocheted bedspreads, handcrafted ceramics, and seasonal decorations transformed the space into something uniquely ours.

In the living room stood the Emerson TV and a rotary phone—symbols of connection: one reaching outward to the world, the other inward to the hearts that mattered most. Goldfish swam in silence, parakeets sang, and the home pulsed with gentle life.

Mommy was stern and truth-telling, yet her love overflowed in action. A pillar of strength and leadership in the Quinton community, she had a special love for children. Perhaps that's why Allah didn't give her biological children—so she could become a mother to *many*.

She organized church plays, summer trips to the beach, and excursions to Washington, D.C., where children marveled at monuments and museums. As a 4-H Club leader, she taught gardening, cooking, sewing, and crafts. She baked towering chocolate layer cakes and celebrated every child's birthday with warmth and song. A fierce fundraiser for church and school, she rallied the women of the community with tireless energy. Once Mommy got an idea, you could trust it would come to life. She was truly a jack of all trades and the Queen Mother of Quinton.

And then there was Daddy—my hero. His spirit was gentle, his kindness unshakable, his presence grounding.

Missie, my little dog, and I would walk the fields and woods with Daddy—whether hunting or tending the garden. Along the way, he taught me about vegetables, trees, birds, and how to recognize danger: poisonous berries, wild animals. Everything he did came with love and purpose

In the garden, Daddy would dig holes and show me how to count, drop seeds in, and gently cover them. He taught me games—checkers, dominoes, card games, tic-tac-toe, baseball, and yo-yo. And every night, he read to me—Bible stories, picture books—and led me in my bedtime prayer:

> 'Now I lay me down to sleep,
> I pray to the Lord my soul to keep.

If I should die before I wake,
I pray to the Lord my soul to take."

Then he'd hug me, tuck me in, and kiss me goodnight.

Daddy's love wasn't just for me. Teenage boys—especially those without fathers—would gather under the big sycamore tree in our yard, talking with Daddy, whom they affectionately called "Bubbie." I was too young to understand their conversations, but I knew this: they found peace, comfort, and wisdom under that tree.

Growing up in the Safe Haven Sanctuary wasn't just a blessing. It was a divine appointment. Mommy and Daddy shaped my life with discipline, devotion, and a depth of love that still holds me steady. They were—and always will be—precious beyond words.

A Home That Welcomes the World

At the Safe Haven Sanctuary, holidays weren't merely celebrated—they pulsed through the air, saturated the spirit, and etched themselves into memory.

Birthdays were sacred. Whenever a village child's special day arrived, Mommy baked her signature chocolate layer cake, its sweet aroma curling through the house like a promise. Children from every corner of the community gathered in the backyard, now transformed into a wonderland of streamers and balloons dancing in the breeze. Sack races, bobbing for apples, and piñatas bursting with treats filled the air with squeals of joy. As we sang the birthday song, the flicker of candles lit up each child's face—reflections of love poured out by Mommy and Daddy's devotion.

Memorial Day brought a tradition of togetherness. Daddy would fire up the grill, the smoky perfume of ribs, chicken, and burgers wafting across the yard. Mommy and her circle of friends prepared creamy potato salad, crisp coleslaw, and warm cornbread—dishes that spoke of care and community. Children chased bubbles and played tag as laughter wove its way through the yard like a second wind.

As dusk fell, cars piled high with lawn chairs and blankets made their way to the **Glen drive-in theater**. There, under the stars, we watched films with popcorn in our laps and the hum of crickets in our ears. It wasn't just a movie—it was belonging under a sky stitched with memory.

The Fourth of July exploded with color and flavor. Mr. Moses Friday—Daddy's lifelong friend and chosen son—anchored the day with a whole-hog roast under the old cedar tree. The scent of seasoned pork mingled with the sharp tang of Mommy's crab pot blend—vinegar, beer, and cayenne—setting mouths to water long before the feast began. Family poured in from New York, embraced in fast-talking tales and belly laughs. Music spilled into the village, lifting hearts and feet alike. As night fell, the porch lights flickered like stars, guiding us into a celebration that lingered deep into the dark.

Thanksgiving was a full-week affair. The elder men and boys hunted with joy, while Mommy orchestrated the kitchen like a conductor. My favorite—sweet potato pie—led a delicious parade: lemon pies, fruitcakes, chocolate cakes, pound cakes. The table gleamed beneath polished glassware and candlelight, with a golden turkey reigning over a court of dressing, greens, jeweled beets, macaroni and cheese, and oven-fresh rolls. Grace wasn't just a prayer—it was the spirit of the season itself, poured out in every gesture.

Christmas hummed with harmony and holy mischief. Daddy and I strung lights with tangled laughter, then crunched through the woods in search of the perfect evergreen, our sacred family ritual. Mommy's holiday table glowed beneath a white crocheted cloth, with holly and cranberries nestled beside flickering candles. Roast turkey, Smithfield ham, mashed potatoes, candied yams, fruitcake, and pie crowned the meal. Even simple gifts—an orange, a handful of nuts, a single peppermint stick—carried wonder. But the true magic of Christmas was togetherness: faith, love, and gratitude, wrapped in memory.

The Sanctuary of Strength, Safety, and Spirit

The Alice and Randolph Brown Safe Haven Sanctuary was more than a house—it was a haven. A refuge crafted not just with timber and nails, but with compassion, resilience, and unwavering faith. Built by my Mommy and Daddy, it stood as a living testament to their belief in the redemptive power of love and community.

Their doors were never closed to those in need. Within those walls, they offered not just shelter, but emotional and spiritual sustenance. Whether comforting a grieving relative, nurturing a child through growing pains, or offering wisdom in moments of confusion, they gave of themselves freely—always with quiet grace and without expectation.

At the heart of the sanctuary was a mission: to lift others up, even in the midst of personal hardship. It was a place where brokenness was met with belief, where second chances were not rare blessings but sacred responsibilities. The soul of the home resided in my parents' conviction that no one was beyond healing, and that love—steady, fierce, and patient—could mend even the most frayed spirit.

Mommy and Daddy embodied dignity and grace. Their gentle strength created a space where people could exhale, be seen, and be restored. They never sought recognition. Their reward was in the quiet transformation of those who passed through their care.

Their legacy still lives and breathes. The Safe Haven Sanctuary remains a beacon—a reminder that the truest homes are not built of stone, but of spirit. And that healing doesn't begin with perfection—it begins with open arms and the courageous decision to love anyway.

Great Great Grandma Tavee Great Great Grandpa Harrison

Mary Frances & Gwen

Uncle Harold Army Days

Great-grandparents
(Nana & Papa)

Mommy, Daddy & Me

The Ida and William Christian
Barn and Farmhouse

Nana & Papa's House

Cousin Ollie & Cousin Beck Moss

Sis Alma Lightfoot

Cousin John Lightfoot

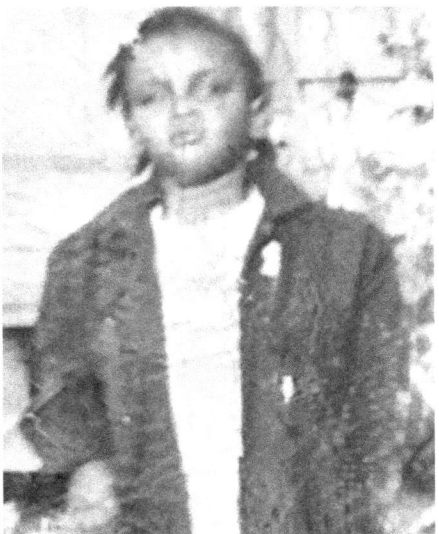

Jean DePriest

Ernest and Alberta Crump

Larry Green: 6 years old

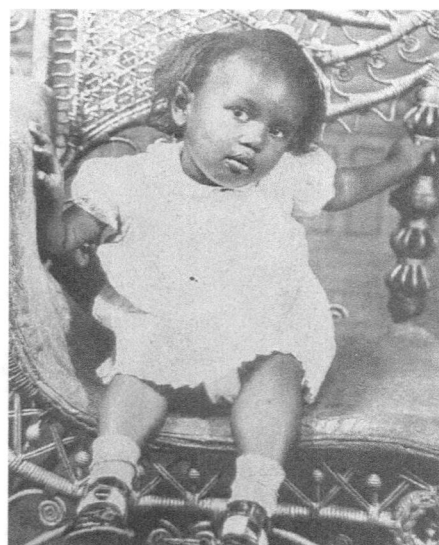

Joan Christian

Vann Christian

Benjamin 'Bennie' Lockley:
6 years old

Mommy & Daddy

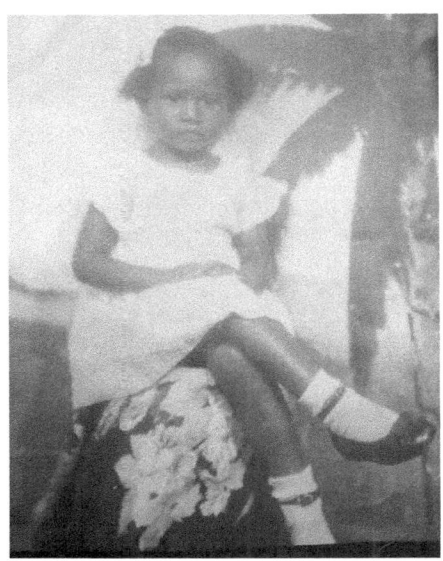

Gwen

CHAPTER 4

UNION BAPTIST: OUR VILLAGE'S SACRED HOME

A Pillow of Faith, Forged in Generations

Less than a mile from the heart of the Christian-Carter-Brown Village stood Union Baptist Church—a radiant beacon of hope and belonging. Its weathered wooden boards, softened by time and steeped in generations of whispered prayers, exuded a quiet warmth that welcomed all who passed through its doors. Sunlight filtered through stained-glass windows, casting a kaleidoscope of color across the sanctuary—where every hymn and every silent plea carried the enduring promise of unity.

A landmark in both presence and purpose, Union Baptist rests on approximately two acres of sacred ground in Quinton, Virginia. Established in the mid-1800s, it was not merely a house of worship, but a living testament to faith, resilience, and the unbreakable spirit of a community that had leaned on it for generations.

From my earliest memories, Union Baptist was more than a church—it was the heartbeat of Quinton. In the tradition of the Black church, it provided spiritual grounding, a pillar of solidarity, and a sanctuary in times of trial. But it was also something more—it was the place where lives intertwined and stories were passed on, a vessel of memory and momentum.

The grounds themselves seemed to breathe with intention. Families gathered there not only to worship, but to live out the sacred rhythms of village life. Children played with unbridled joy, their laughter echoing off the church walls, while elders shared wisdom beneath sun-dappled trees. Sunday services were never only about sermons—they were about connection, culture, and the weaving together of kin and neighbor.

Within those wooden walls, every joy and sorrow was spoken aloud—cradled in hymns, lifted by prayer, and wrapped in the steady faith of a people who believed in healing, even when the world outside offered little of it.

Guiding Lights of Union Baptist and the Legacy of Faithful Leadership

Among Union Baptist's most enduring guiding lights was Mr. Lanza Minor—a pillar of quiet strength and unwavering conviction. As Sunday School Superintendent, he led with deep faith and purpose. His close bond with my Papa, a fellow deacon, reflected the kind of kinship that fortified the church's spiritual foundation. Deacon Minor believed wholeheartedly in nurturing the next generation of leaders who would carry Union Baptist into the future.

One of the most defining moments of his forward-thinking spirit came during a Sunday School gathering when he rose and boldly recommended that my cousin Bill—just 15 years old—be appointed Sunday School Superintendent. It was a revolutionary proposal for the time. The room fell into a hush, not from disbelief, but from awe. Deacon Minor's wisdom and authority were so deeply respected that the congregation embraced the idea without hesitation.

Under his mentorship, young Bill thrived in the role—leading with maturity beyond his years until his high school graduation, when he left to serve in the U.S. Army. That single act of trust changed more than just Bill's life; it left an indelible mark on our church community. It taught us the power of believing in our youth and the importance of passing the torch with intentional grace.

When Bill moved on, Mr. Carl Christian stepped seamlessly into the role of Superintendent. In his late twenties, full of charisma and vision, he brought renewed energy to the Sunday School program. But his leadership extended far beyond the church's four walls.

Under Mr. Christian's guidance, we traveled to Washington, D.C., marveling at monuments and meandering through the National Zoo. During the summer heat, he organized beach trips with tireless dedication—rallying parents, securing transportation, and ensuring no child was left behind.

Because of segregation, our beach choices were limited to Black-owned retreats like Mark Haven Beach in Essex County, Buckroe Beach in Hampton, and Dandridge Lake in Mechanicsville. Still, the joy we experienced was uncontainable. These outings became bridges— connecting us to other Black congregations from Henrico, Charles City, Hanover, King and Queen, and King William counties. It was fellowship in its truest form: joy-soaked, heart-lifting, and woven with shared resilience.

Mr. Christian also championed the Varina-Fairfield Sunday School Union. Every fifth Sunday, churches from New Kent and Henrico gathered in spirited unity. After the business portion concluded, a child between five and ten years old was chosen to recite a Bible verse before the congregations. The applause was warm and thunderous, and each child received a King James Bible.

I still remember mine.

Trembling with a blend of nerves and pride, I recited *Matthew 5:1–5*. That verse, that moment, remains etched in my spirit—a quiet yet powerful affirmation of my young faith.

And then came summer, ushering in the sacred joy of Vacation Bible School. For one whole week each year, Union Baptist became a wonderland of spiritual discovery. Children arrived from all corners of Quinton, their shoes dusty, their eyes bright. Our first VBS Superintendent, Ms. Annie Oliver, was a woman of many gifts—Sunday School teacher, pianist for both Union Baptist and Rising Mt. Zion in Sandston, and a nurturer of countless young souls. Her kindness filled every classroom and echoed in every piano key she struck.

When Ms. Oliver stepped down, the mantle passed to Rev. Elmore Warren—a spirited young minister fresh from Virginia Union's School of Theology. He brought a modern vitality to our lessons. I'll never forget the day he taught us the meaning of *omnipotent, omnipresent*, and *omniscient*. His voice rang with clarity and conviction. More than sixty years later, that lesson still lives in my mind like it was yesterday.

So what made VBS so special? It was more than Bible stories and crafts. It was our escape from chores, our reunion with classmates, our time to shine. Each class filled our minds and hearts with lessons, love, and laughter. On the final day, we showcased our creations and received certificates—small in size, but enormous in meaning. Proof that we were growing—in faith, in knowledge, and in community.

A Journey Through Fellowship and Baptism

The fourth Sunday in August was reserved for something sacred: the Union Baptist Homecoming Revival. On that day, the very air seemed to hum with anticipation. People traveled from miles around to reunite with loved ones and rekindle old connections. Even the blazing summer sun couldn't dim the spirit of the gathering. It was part worship service, part family reunion, and wholly a celebration of faith, tradition, and the enduring strength of our village.

The church grounds transformed into a vibrant scene of fellowship and festivity. For days, the ladies of the church had worked tirelessly to prepare an unforgettable feast. When they arrived, they came dressed in their Sunday best—elegant hats perched just so, dresses coordinated with care—turning the day into a dazzling showcase of beauty and pride.

Long tables stretched beneath the shade trees beside the church, covered with dish after dish of beloved recipes. Each cook had their specialty. Mommy's table was the destination for those craving sweet potato pie. Sis Alma's corn pudding and rolls were the stuff of legend. Aunt Martha's potato salad never lasted long. The list of culinary masters went on: Mrs. Henrietta Christian, Mrs. Mary Lou Williams, Cousin Annie, Cousin Rebecca, Mrs. Mary Christian, Mrs. Mary Becoat, Mrs. Elizabeth Johnson, Mrs. Martha Christian, Mrs. Mary Washington, Mrs. Mary Minor, and Mrs. Madeline Willoughby. Their food was more than nourishment—it was memory, tradition, and love served by the plateful.

Inside the sanctuary, music filled every corner as the old piano and organ came to life beneath the skilled hands of musicians who played beautifully by ear. Even when the harmonies wavered, the congregation's voices carried the rhythm forward with that familiar *patty-foot beat*—a cadence passed down through generations. On sweltering days, with windows wide open and no breeze in sight, the ushers moved with grace and care, handing out fans donated by the local funeral home—an iconic comfort in Black church gatherings everywhere.

Then came the fourth Sunday in September—our community's sacred welcome to fall and the day set aside for one of the most meaningful events of the church calendar: the baptism of those who, during revival, made the life-altering decision to accept Christ as their personal Lord and Savior.

I remember my own baptism as vividly as if it happened yesterday.

It was a Tuesday night in August 1962. I was just eleven years old. Rev. Dr. Clifton Whitaker, Sr., the revivalist that year, delivered a sermon so powerful it stirred something deep within me. That night, I knew. I wanted to give my life to Christ. I ran home to Nana, heart full, and told her the news. Her eyes softened with joy, and she smiled. "If it's God's will," she said, "I will be there for your baptism."

And she was.

I was baptized in the gentle, flowing waters of the Chickahominy River at Bottoms Bridge by Rev. Howard Wallace and my great-grandfather, Papa. Nana stood on the riverbank, her presence as steady as the faith that had carried our family through generations. I remember the cool embrace of the water, the hush of the crowd, the quiet authority of the hands that guided me under and back up again.

In that sacred moment, I was reborn—swaddled in legacy, rooted in faith, and ready to walk the path of devotion.

It remains one of the most treasured memories of my life. I can still feel Nana's pride from the shore, her gaze holding the weight of our past and the promise of everything to come. Her first great-grandchild, beginning a journey she had prayed for long before I ever knew to dream it.

From Youthful Roles to Lifelong Callings

Christmastime at Union Baptist Church shimmered with joy, community, and reverence. The annual Christmas plays were cherished traditions—a sacred retelling of the birth of Jesus that brought the entire congregation together in awe and celebration. Preparations were a labor of love, with Ms. Mary Lou and Mommy carefully stitching costumes that transformed us into angels, shepherds, and wise men.

I can still see Mommy bending coat hangers into delicate halos and wings, then wrapping them in white cloth until they glowed with heavenly shimmer. The boys wore hand-sewn robes in rich jewel tones and homemade crowns, stepping into their roles with a sense of wonder and pride.

No child was ever left out. The elders of the church, guardians of tradition and tenderness, prepared bushels of apples and oranges, then filled brown paper bags with a mix of nuts and hard candy for each child. The scent alone—a mingling of citrus and sugar—was enough to mark the holiday as sacred. And every little one received a wrapped gift: a pair of socks and gloves tucked neatly into festive paper. These were no grand gestures, yet they embodied profound love, care, and belonging.

Every second Sunday of the month was Youth Sunday—a sacred rite of passage. On those mornings, the young people led the entire service. We sang in the choir, read Scripture aloud, led prayers, and ushered guests with pride. These roles stretched us. They nurtured responsibility, fostered confidence, and quietly prepared us for the callings ahead.

I still smile at the memory of my cousin Larry's first time leading. Like many of us, he was "voluntold" by Mommy to step up—dressed in a stiff brown corduroy suit that carried the weight of tradition, expectation, and nerves. Larry was painfully shy, and his stutter often wrapped around his words like tangled vines. As he stood before the congregation, the sanctuary held its breath. And then—miraculously—his voice emerged clear, steady, and full of quiet conviction. In that moment, something sacred happened. A breakthrough. A beginning.

Larry would go on to become a minister, eventually pastoring two churches with strength and compassion. The same voice that once trembled would later stir congregations with clarity and power. Union

Baptist gave him—and so many others—a place to find their voice, their courage, and their calling.

Stories like his weren't rare. The church was holy ground for transformation. It was a place where whispered encouragements and loving nudges became seeds of leadership. Whether we were reading Scripture, singing a solo, preparing food under the pine trees, or simply serving water on a hot revival day—each act became sacred preparation for something greater.

Looking back, it's clear: Union Baptist wasn't just a church we attended. It was a church that lived inside us. Its people, traditions, and rhythms of worship formed the bedrock of our identity. The elders didn't merely pray with us—they prepared us. Through the changing seasons of revival, baptism, celebration, and communion, they passed down more than memories.

They passed down legacy.

Union Baptist Church

My Baptism

Me & Momma
(My baptism)

Papa, Me, and Nana
(Baptism Day)

Bill - Sunday School
Superintendent(15 years old)

Larry
Union Baptist Homecoming

CHAPTER 5

EMBARKING ON A LIFELONG ODYSSEY OF LEARNING

Charting My First-Grade Journey

My formal educational journey began in the fall of 1957 at a humble Rosenwald one-room schoolhouse—modest in size, monumental in influence. Nestled just steps from Union Baptist Church in New Kent County, Virginia, it was more than a school. It was a sacred threshold: a place where dreams took root and vision turned to action. We knew it as Quinton Elementary School, though its history reached far deeper.

The heartbeat of that history lay in the partnership between Julius Rosenwald, the Sears, Roebuck & Co. magnate, and Booker T. Washington of Tuskegee Institute. Together, they launched a revolutionary initiative to fund and build schools for Black children across the segregated South. Between 1912 and 1937, nearly 5,000 Rosenwald schools were established, with almost 400 in Virginia alone. In our village, Union Baptist Church donated the land for what began as the Quinton Colored School—an act of faith, vision, and fierce commitment to our future.

The excitement I felt on that first day of school is still vivid. The journey alone felt like a grand adventure. Papa—our beloved bus driver—was always the first smiling face we saw. Children from every corner of the Christian-Carter-Brown Village gathered at Nana and Papa's home each morning, climbing aboard bus #25. I remember Papa warming up the bus on chilly mornings, filling it with comfort and care before we ever set foot inside.

Beneath my joy, though, flickered a child's vulnerability. One morning, a neighborhood boy named David Morris tried to bully me. But before fear could settle in, my cousin Ida stepped in—fierce and swift, a mother hen in motion. The look on David's face said it all. Family stood as my shield, and no one dared test that bond.

Quinton Elementary was a two-room schoolhouse serving grades one through seven, though in my first year, only grades one through three were offered. Our classroom was more than a space—it was a family. Names like Diane Williams, Daniel Morris, Steven Minor, Luke Christian, Robert Brown, Bernard Minor, David Terry, Carolyn Christian, Mamie Crump, and Carolyn Pryor are stitched into the fabric of my early education. Together, we grew, learned, and became.

At the helm of our tiny universe stood Ms. Edna Johnson—our teacher, guide, and surrogate mother. Tasked with teaching multiple grades at once, she moved among us with grace and mastery. She'd begin with the first graders, shift to the second, then the third, ensuring each child felt seen and supported. I often finished my work early and sat quietly, absorbing the older students' lessons. In those moments, I learned more than academics—I learned patience, curiosity, and the unspoken art of communal learning.

Ms. Johnson had no children of her own, but poured a mother's love into each of us. A gifted artist, she transformed our classroom into a canvas of imagination. Her drawings adorned the walls like windows into her soul. She led us on nature walks, where the world became our textbook. I remember collecting tadpoles from Mr. Black's Pond and watching in awe as they slowly transformed into frogs. In the fall, we gathered leaves in every hue; she turned them into breathtaking collages. Winter brought hand-cut snowflakes that fluttered above us like delicate dreams.

During recess, our voices rose in joyful chorus as we sang, *"Ring Around the Rosie," "Old MacDonald," "If You're Happy and You Know It," "Row, Row, Row Your Boat,"* and *"The Mulberry Bush."* The playground was our theater, our sanctuary, and our classroom.

Ms. Johnson's dedication extended beyond the schoolhouse walls. The mothers in our community were always ready to uplift her. I especially remember her birthday—March 17, St. Patrick's Day—when Mommy, Ms. Mary Lou, and Ms. Henrietta would surprise her with a cake and warm celebration. Her tears of gratitude spoke volumes. In our village, teaching was not a job—it was a sacred trust. And our gratitude flowed freely to those who upheld it.

This early chapter of my life—full of learning, creativity, and collective care—planted seeds I carry still. It taught me that education thrives not just on textbooks, but on love, resilience, beauty, and community. In that tiny schoolhouse beside our sacred church, I learned lessons far beyond reading and arithmetic.

I learned how to become.

Transformative Steps Toward Belonging

My second year of school unfolded against a backdrop of profound change—not just for me, but for every Black child in New Kent County. In 1958, the opening of George W. Watkins Elementary School was more than an expansion of public education. It was a beacon—standing tall along Route 33 (now Route 249), beside George W. Watkins High School in Quinton, Virginia—as a promise that a brighter future was within reach. It welcomed children from Lanexa, Mountcastle, Tunstall, Cumberland, Plum Point, Barhamsville, and Providence Forge, gathering us under one hopeful roof.

Each morning, our journey began aboard the big yellow bus—a moving tapestry of laughter, nerves, and shared dreams. With Papa behind the wheel, his steady hands and warm smile made even the most anxious child feel safe. He wasn't merely our driver; he was our protector, our kin, guiding his grandchildren, great-grandchildren, nieces, nephews, and neighbors with quiet pride.

The bus ride itself was a ritual of connection. Each stop brought new faces and deeper bonds. First came the Hewletts—Edna, Russell, Bobby, and Earl—eager and full of energy. Then, children from the Annabelle Morris Dwelling and the Mamie and Arthur Christian Villa joined us: David and Daniel Morris, – Shirley and Ernest Ellis, Jr., Edward Christian, Barbara and Emma Shelton. As we made our way down Route 33, the Bassett children—Elnora, Roscoe, Irene, Edna, and Edwin—climbed aboard with quiet grace. Milton and Maxine Davis followed, then Joyce and Walda Braxton, their waves full of light. The Thompson trio—Yvonne, Hugo, and Phillip—brought laughter, followed by Brenda and Gordon Thompson. Jerome Johnson, raised by his grandparents, embodied the strength of generational love. Our last stop was at the home of Ms. Oraphine and Bennie Crump, where Bennie Jr. and his cousin Bertha Watkins, bright-eyed and full of curiosity, completed our sacred caravan.

That bus was never just transportation—it was communion. A mobile sanctuary where every mile stitched us tighter together, a living reminder that in times of transition, our community held firm.

When we arrived at the school, our hearts fluttered with anticipation. The teachers stood waiting with clipboards in hand. And there, as familiar and beloved as ever, was Ms. Edna Johnson. When she called my name, joy rushed in. She took our small hands and led us into classrooms that felt immediately safe and warm. But this time, most of my former classmates had been assigned to Ms. Mary Murray's class. My new classmates hailed from distant communities—Barhamsville, Lanexa and Tunstall, Mountcastle, Cumberland and, Plum Point. At first, their unfamiliar faces stirred unease. But new friendships soon took root, and I began carving out a place for myself in this growing tapestry.

That year also brought a shift within my own family. My younger sister, Pinkie, came to live with me. She entered first grade under Ms. Alberta Coleman's care, but early struggles revealed the learning challenges she faced. One day, I watched as Pinkie crawled across the classroom floor, her mouth stained purple from a chewed pencil. Ms. Coleman called me over gently, encouraging Pinkie to rise and try again. That moment remains etched in my heart—fragile, tender, and full of sisterly love.

That summer, between second and third grade, brought an unexpected blessing. Ms. Thelma Watkins, the kind-hearted school librarian and wife of our principal, Dr. George W. Watkins, invited me to help in the library. Dr. Watkins himself picked me up. I spent the day shelving books, soaking in the quiet magic of that sacred space. Ms. Watkins shared her lunch with me and tucked a bit of change in my hand— small gestures that seeded in me a lifelong respect for responsibility, generosity, and work done with love.

But joy was soon shadowed by grief. Late that summer of 1959, as the third grade approached, Sis Alma turned on WANT—the Black-owned radio station—and heard devastating news. Ms. Johnson and her brother had been killed in a car accident on Route 60 while returning from a visit in Charles City County. Sis Alma called Mommy, her voice shaking with sorrow.

Mommy took me to their double funeral at Elam Baptist Church, in Charles City, Virginia. Dr. Watkins delivered a heartfelt eulogy that soothed our aching spirits. As I sat quietly among mourners who had also been touched by Ms. Johnson's boundless love, I whispered goodbye. Even now, more than sixty-five years later, tears rise at the memory of that loss. She was more than a teacher. She was the beginning of so many beautiful things.

Igniting the Spark of Discovery

On the first day of third grade, my steps were hesitant, my nerves fluttering. But as I scanned the hallways, familiar faces smiled back at me, and comfort returned. At the classroom door, Mrs. Helen Burrell and Mrs. Idelle Cooper greeted students with clipboards and warmth. I found my name on Mrs. Burrell's list, and relief washed over me. Several of my second-grade classmates had also been assigned to her class, and something about that felt exactly right.

Mrs. Burrell moved with quiet strength, her slight limp no match for her energy or presence. She became a shaping force in my life. In her classroom, the world opened wider.

She introduced us to Paul Laurence Dunbar, the poet whose verses lit the fire of expression in generations of Black children. Her favorite was "Possum," and she recited it with such rhythm and passion that we could almost hear the footsteps of its subject. Learning about Dunbar—the first Black American to earn a living as a writer—planted a dream in us: that our voices, too, had power.

Mrs. Burrell and Mrs. Cooper also expanded our education beyond textbooks. They took us on unforgettable field trips to the Pamunkey and Mattaponi Indian Reservations in King William County. These weren't just school excursions. They were cultural awakenings. We learned about the rich history of Virginia's Native peoples, walked in the legacy of the Powhatan Confederacy, and glimpsed the world of Pocahontas and her people.

But what set Mrs. Burrell apart was the way she made us feel seen. Her reward system turned achievement into celebration. Four pieces of candy for an A. Three for a B. Two for a C. Even a D earned a small, encouraging treat. Under her care, failure felt nearly impossible. Her method wasn't indulgent—it was motivational. She reminded us daily that we mattered, that effort bore fruit, and that every child held potential waiting to bloom.

That third year was transformative. It blended literature, history, compassion, and exploration into an education that transcended books. Every lesson lit a spark. Every experience became a steppingstone. And every gesture from our teachers reminded us that we were capable, valued, and never alone.

A Window into a World of Wonders

Time moved swiftly as I entered my fourth year of elementary school. Our new teachers, Ms. Helen Watkins and Ms. Inez Bailey, greeted us with warm smiles that transformed the classroom into a sanctuary of curiosity and care. I was placed in Ms. Watkins' class, where my assigned seat by the window gave me more than just a view—it gave me a quiet tether to the world beyond Route 33. As I watched people stroll by and cars hum along the road, I felt connected to something larger than myself.

Within that classroom, a new marvel made its appearance: the rotary telephone. It seemed almost magical. Ms. Watkins placed the sleek, black model on her desk, and I watched in silent awe. The round dial gleamed beneath the soft classroom lights, each number etched into its face like a secret waiting to be unlocked. As Ms. Watkins demonstrated how to use it, the gentle clicks and whirls of the dial felt like music—an intricate rhythm that echoed with the promise of distant voices and untold stories.

Each rotation of the dial was like casting a small, wondrous spell. The clicking sound as it returned to its place was a heartbeat of progress, one that stirred both curiosity and possibility. For us, it wasn't just a phone—it was a symbol of transformation. Bell Telephone Company had begun installing lines throughout the county, and my parents were among the first in our Village to have one in their home. That knowledge filled me with a deep, childlike pride. We weren't just receiving a new device—we were becoming connected to a wider, more mysterious world.

The telephone's arrival came with a thrill of mystery. Ms. Watkins explained "party lines"—shared phone lines that carried the voices of our neighbors and, occasionally, voices from places we had never seen. Each time she demonstrated its use, it felt like a portal was opening, reaching across fences, across counties, across realities. What once belonged to others was now in our hands. That black rotary phone, with its patient dial and gentle hum, became more than a tool—it was a declaration that progress had found its way to Quinton.

Still, the year wasn't without sorrow. That same fall, Aunt Martha and her family moved to Richmond, taking my classmate and cousin Jackie with them. The absence of her sisters—Erselle, Ida, Shortie, and Millie—left a hollow stillness in our corner of the Village. Bill had already graduated and joined the Army, and the loneliness my sister and I felt deepened in their absence.

These personal shifts unfolded alongside the growing rumble of the American Civil Rights Movement. Though I was still just a young Black girl in a small classroom, the weight of injustice was impossible to ignore. I often looked out the window and saw Dr. George W. Watkins walking briskly along the sidewalk, his head bowed beneath burdens only adults seemed to carry. I began to understand, in fragments and feelings, what it meant to live in a world where being Black meant carrying extra weight.

Our school, though filled with warmth and effort, bore the marks of inequality. There were days when we had to close—not for holidays, but because the heat didn't work or water had backed up from a failing system. Our books were hand-me-downs from white schools, their worn covers and marked-up pages quietly speaking the language of second-class status. The desks were scratched, the devices outdated, the message unmistakable.

And yet, in the middle of it all—this strange dance of wonder and injustice—we learned to find joy. We learned to adapt. We found beauty in shared moments and strength in what we built together. The year was a patchwork of discovery and disillusionment, each thread weaving a more honest picture of the world.

From the rotary phone to the reality of racial inequality, from Ms. Watkins' lessons to the ache of saying goodbye, that fourth-grade year taught me not only how to learn—but why we must. It ignited something lasting: a sense of watchfulness, a hunger for justice, and a resilience that would carry me through many more chapters yet to come.

A Journey Through Fear and Endurance

Fifth grade began with a heavy dread that settled deep in my chest and tightened with each passing day. The thought of being assigned to Mrs. Eva John Brown's class was almost too much to bear. Older students had whispered their warnings in hushed, reverent tones: she was strict, unbending, a force to be feared. Her weapon of choice—the infamous wooden paddle ominously dubbed the "Board of Education"—was more than legend; it was a real and looming threat. In a time when corporal punishment wasn't just tolerated but expected by most parents, her reign over the classroom was absolute.

From the moment I stepped into her room, a quiet terror took root inside me. The weight of her authority silenced my voice, dulled my curiosity, and shrank my presence. I learned quickly that the best chance of surviving the year was to make myself small—nearly invisible. The classroom became a place of vigilance, not wonder. Learning turned into an act of quiet endurance. There was no room for joy, no space for exploration, only the persistent pressure to avoid being noticed.

Two moments from that year remain etched in my memory with painful clarity.

The first was the quiet unraveling of Jimmy (James, Jr.) Christian—one of the brightest lights in our school. He was sharp, thoughtful, and effortlessly gifted. His presence once lit the room, his confidence and kindness admired by all. But that year, sorrow came for him. His father died of lung cancer, and in the wake of that loss, Jimmy changed. The twinkle in his eyes dimmed. His laughter faded into silence. We watched helplessly as grief slowly hollowed out the spark that once defined him. It was the first time I saw how mourning could change someone's walk, their voice, their sense of self.

The second memory is one I still carry in the pit of my stomach. One afternoon, I scribbled something hastily on a scrap of paper, crossed out my name, and left it on a nearby desk, intending to throw it away later. But Mrs. Brown saw it first. Her eyes narrowed, her voice sharp as she asked, "Who put this piece of paper here?" Panic surged through me like a tidal wave. I froze. I couldn't bring myself to confess. The paper felt like a criminal offense in her hands. The next day, in front of the entire class, she announced: "I know who left that paper—but I won't say until the end of the school year."

From that moment on, each day became a quiet torment. I lived beneath a cloud of impending doom, dreading the day she might call my name. Her every glance sent my heart into spirals. What should have been a year of growth became instead a daily ritual of anxiety. There was no learning in that space—only surviving.

And survive, I did. I endured the year, but not without cost. That classroom marked my first intimate encounter with trauma—the kind that doesn't bruise the skin, but scars the spirit. I learned how fear, when left unchecked, can shrink a child's world. I saw how authority, when wielded without compassion, can harden the softest parts of us.

Yet in that suffocating season, I also discovered something quietly powerful: survival is its own kind of triumph. In the face of a system that rewarded silence and punished vulnerability, simply making it through the year was an act of defiance. Though my confidence dimmed under her watch, a small ember remained—ready, one day, to be rekindled by gentler hands.

Navigating a Year of Growth and Self-Discovery

Sixth grade ushered in a quiet transformation—both within the classroom and in the hidden chambers of our lives. The air felt charged with the winds of change, sometimes exhilarating, sometimes disorienting. It was a year when friendships deepened, lessons took on richer meaning, and tragedy arrived in a form that would never fully release its hold.

Our teachers were Mrs. Marjorie Carter and Ms. Julia Brown, and I felt deeply blessed to be placed in Mrs. Carter's class. She carried herself with a gentle dignity—soft-spoken, warm, and deeply nurturing. Her presence felt like a protective blanket, a calming force that made our classroom feel like a sanctuary from the challenges beyond its walls. She played a pivotal role in the life of our classmate and my dear friend, Ernestine Malloy—her husband's niece, whom she raised as her own. That act alone was a quiet testimony to Mrs. Carter's immense capacity for love.

Sixth grade was also a season of awakening. Puberty crept in with its blushes and questions, stirring a new awareness of our bodies, how others perceived us, and the insecurities that shadowed our growing minds. In a gesture both thoughtful and wise, Mrs. Carter and Ms. Brown gathered the girls one afternoon and spoke with quiet candor about menstruation, hygiene, and self-care. Their approach was tender, informative, and dignified. Where our parents might have struggled to find the words, they offered clarity and compassion, leaving us better prepared—and more deeply seen.

But even as the year offered moments of learning and self-discovery, it also brought devastation.

On January 10, 1963, tragedy arrived like a thief in the night, devastating the heart of our Village. That frigid morning, beneath a blanket of snow, fire swept through the beloved Harrison and Octavia ("Tavee") Christian Homestead. In just minutes, flames consumed everything.

Before the fire, the homestead was a symbol of endurance. When cousins Rebecca and Ollie moved to Mountcastle in Providence Forge, Ms. Elizabeth Minor and her family took shelter within its walls. A hardworking single mother, Ms. Elizabeth cleaned houses and ironed for local families, providing for her children with steadfast determination. Her older children—Melinda, Henrietta, and Benjamin—were already forging their own paths, while Phyllis, Roland, Evelyn, and Bernard remained at home, doing what they could to sustain the household. Phyllis and Roland had even sacrificed their education to work.

Each morning before dawn, Ms. Elizabeth, Phyllis, and Roland left for their jobs. Young Bernard, still in elementary school, joined us at the bus stop, leaving behind a house filled with sleeping teenage mothers and their little ones. Evelyn remained behind to care for her children, along with Roland's girlfriend, Ann Morris, and her baby. Ann's cousin, Virginia Christian, lived there as well, caring for her own infant son.

Then, the fire came.

Without warning, flames engulfed the wooden house with terrifying speed. There were no sirens, no fire trucks, no rescue. Everyone inside perished—except Virginia. She escaped physically unharmed, but the trauma of survival etched itself into her soul. The weight of witnessing such horror would never lift.

The loss reverberated through the Village like a funeral bell, tolling a sorrow that would never truly fade. Grief hovered over us, thick as smoke, long after the embers died.

Yet even in grief, life continued its steady march forward. In June 1963, a more hopeful milestone arrived: my cousin Larry graduated from high school. His graduation was more than a ceremony; it was a triumph of perseverance. Larry was never the loudest or most popular student—he wasn't drawn to crowds or the thrill of the court. Instead, he found solace in books, tucked away in corners where ideas lived. His hard work was rewarded with an $800 scholarship to Virginia Union University. He earned it not through flash, but through quiet, consistent determination.

Watching Larry walk across that stage, diploma in hand, I felt a mix of pride and melancholy. His departure left a quiet ache in my heart. But his journey illuminated something essential: success is not always loud. Sometimes, it's found in the quiet hours, the unnoticed effort, the books devoured in solitude. Mentors like Dr. and Mrs. Watkins had seen this in Larry early on—not just his intellect, but his discipline. They celebrated him not for accolades, but for the depth of his character.

His story taught me that growth often requires release. As Larry stepped forward into his new chapter, I was left to reflect on my own path— on what it meant to hold space for grief and gratitude, for hope and heartache.

That year left an indelible mark on my spirit. It was a season of sorrow, yes—but also one of awakening. The Village had shown me that resilience wasn't always thunderous. Sometimes it came in the steady rhythm of ordinary days, in the quiet strength of endurance, in the lessons whispered between loss and triumph.

And when I think of that year—the fire, the friendship, the farewell—I remember this: though the flames took much, they could not consume what mattered most. The fire within us to endure, to learn, and to rise burned even brighter. It still does.

A Year That Changed Everything

The year 1963 unfolded as a national reckoning—a moment when America stood at a crossroads, teetering between the promise of progress and the weight of deep-rooted injustice. The Civil Rights Movement surged forward with fierce determination, its presence felt in every protest march, courtroom battle, and impassioned speech. That summer, Dr. Martin Luther King Jr. stood beneath the blistering August sun at the Lincoln Memorial and gave voice to a generation's longing. His "I Have a Dream" speech soared across the Mall, echoing through time and igniting hope that had long been buried beneath the rubble of oppression.

Yet for every stride forward, resistance swelled. Riots broke out in response to the Vietnam War, exposing a generation's unrest. Cold War anxieties simmered just beneath the surface, casting long shadows of nuclear dread. These national tensions did not remain distant—they rippled into our own small community, finding their way into family conversations, church meetings, and the determined actions of local heroes.

In New Kent County, the spirit of the movement pulsed through the efforts of leaders like Dr. Calvin Green, Deacon Nathaniel Lewis,

Deacon William Brown, Deacon Samuel Crump, and my own Papa—Deacon William Christian. Alongside devoted women like Mrs. Oraphine Crump, Mrs. Julia Taylor, Mrs. Alease Smith and my mother Alice Brown, they met in the pews and fellowship halls of our churches, mapping out strategies not just to resist injustice but to build something better. They were architects of transformation, constructing change with conviction and unwavering faith.

Mommy and Papa were deeply woven into this sacred work. Civic League and NAACP meetings became a regular part of our lives, and they ensured I was there—not just to sit, but to listen, to absorb. Even as a child, I sensed the gravity of what I was witnessing. In those crowded rooms filled with purpose, I learned that activism was more than protest—it was love in action, a courageous investment in future generations.

And then came November 22, 1963.

The assassination of President John F. Kennedy hit like a gut punch. The news exploded across television and radio, flooding homes and hearts with disbelief. We watched in stunned silence as the nation mourned, our hope momentarily unmoored. Jacqueline Kennedy stood beside Lyndon B. Johnson, her bloodstained pink suit a jarring, unforgettable image. The loss felt personal. Kennedy had come to symbolize the possibility of change—and now, that future seemed to evaporate before our eyes.

In the midst of national mourning and sweeping unrest, seventh grade became its own kind of upheaval. My body and mind shifted, often without warning. That summer, at twelve years old, I experienced my first menstrual cycle—what I would later call "a visit from Aunt Flo." But there was no celebration or ceremony. Mommy, quiet and reserved, simply handed me the necessary supplies. No words. No instruction.

No comfort. I was left to interpret this passage into womanhood on my own.

When school resumed, I found myself in Mr. Phillip Battle's class. He was competent, yes, but rigid—a man of precision rather than presence. In his classroom, discipline ruled, and emotional nuance had no place. After the weight of Mrs. Eva John Brown's rule in fifth grade, I had hoped for something softer. Instead, I found structure without warmth.

One day, in the middle of class, my period arrived—unexpected and undeniable. I raised my hand, anxiety blooming in my chest, and politely asked to go to the restroom. Mr. Battle's response was sharp: "Absolutely not." I tried again, more urgently. He refused again, irritation bristling in his voice. And then, something rose within me—quiet but unyielding. I stood up and, with more resolve than I knew I had, told him I was leaving the room, permission or not.

For a moment, silence reigned. Mr. Battle, caught off guard, said nothing more. I left, shaken but proud. That was the first time I had truly stood my ground, not in rebellion but in reclamation of dignity. A small act, yes—but it changed me.

As the school year drew to a close, the focus turned to graduation. June 1964 brought our final elementary ceremony—a warm Friday evening filled with nervous smiles and satin shoes. The girls wore crisp white dresses, nylons, and polished heels. The boys stood tall in suits and ties. As Ms. Delores Tupponce played "Pomp and Circumstance," we walked with hearts pounding, not just from excitement, but from the gravity of it all. We weren't just leaving a school building—we were crossing a threshold.

That evening marked more than the end of seventh grade. It was the beginning of independence, a quiet awakening to the responsibilities of growing up Black in America, in a time when history turned its pages faster than we could read them. The events of 1963 had etched themselves into me—Dr. King's soaring dream, the grief of a fallen president, the silence of a mother, the unexpected defiance of a young girl, the steady pulse of justice moving through our churches.

And as I stepped forward into the uncharted waters of adolescence and high school, I carried those memories—not as burdens, but as beacons. They lit my way and reminded me that no matter how uncertain the future, I had already begun to find my voice.

Prayers and Prophets: Legacies That Still Speak

In the fall of 1967, during my sophomore year of high school, courage took on a sacred hue as our family faced one of its most heart-wrenching transitions. Our beloved Nana—the spiritual matriarch, our unshakable compass—fell gravely ill and was admitted to the hospital. Even as her body weakened, her spirit remained incandescent. Her prayers echoed down the sterile corridors, full of praise, power, and purpose. On December 6, she made her final transition, walking faithfully toward the promise of her Lord and Savior. In leaving us, Nana did more than pass away—she passed down. She handed us a legacy stitched with resilience, reverence, and a steadfast belief in divine presence.

At the time, I couldn't fully grasp the depth of her devotion. As a girl, I stood quietly in the glow of her faith, awed but unaware. Only now, with the benefit of years and reflection, do I understand what those prayers truly were—declarations. Of love. Of faith. Of hope. Her voice became a spiritual inheritance, its cadence still reverberating through my days. Even now, when I close my eyes, I can almost hear her—petitioning, praising, proclaiming. She wasn't just praying *for* us. She was *planting* something within us.

Nana's quiet strength fortified me in ways I would only come to understand when tested by storms outside the safety of her home. Grief, I've learned, tunes the soul—it sharpens empathy, aligns personal sorrow with the deeper tremors of the world. Just four months after her passing, another blow came—one that shook the soul of a nation.

On April 4, 1968, Rev. Dr. Martin Luther King Jr. was assassinated. The news cracked the air like thunder. The voice of the movement— unwavering in justice, grounded in peace, radical in hope—was silenced. Or so it seemed. Cities erupted. The streets burned. The world tilted on its axis. The grief was familiar, but this time it bore the weight of millions.

Through it all, I held tighter to Nana's prayers. I heard them differently now—as if their echoes rose with the cries of a mourning people. As the nation bent beneath sorrow and outrage, her words returned to me not as comfort alone, but as marching orders. As survival strategy. As strength.

That spring, I understood something vital: adversity doesn't always roar. Sometimes it prays. Sometimes it whispers. Sometimes it simply *endures*.

Both Nana and Dr. King lived this truth. One waged her battles in quiet rooms with folded hands and lifted eyes. The other thundered from pulpits and protest lines. But both left legacies rooted in unwavering conviction. One taught me how to rise through faith, the other how to stand through fire.

And together, they became part of the foundation upon which I would build a life—not untouched by sorrow, but shaped by it. Not immune to loss, but led by love through every valley. Their legacies—woven into spirit and spine—still speak. And I am still listening.

A Passage of Courage, Identity, Adversity, and Triumph Over Adversity

High school marked the beginning of a profound metamorphosis—not only within me, but across a nation wrestling to redefine itself. The

1960s were a reckoning. America stood at a crossroads, its deep-rooted injustices laid bare by the relentless tide of the Civil Rights Movement. As I stepped into these formative years, I felt the pull of two competing realities: the structured path mapped for me since childhood, and the emerging call to chart my own course in a world shifting underfoot.

Education, I came to realize, was never just about mastering content. It was about discovering identity. It was about recognizing knowledge as both shield and sword.

Walking through the halls of George W. Watkins High School felt like entering a living archive of Black excellence. The walls, adorned with portraits of legendary figures and graduating classes dating back to 1950, bore silent witness to generations of struggle and triumph. In a nation still fractured by segregation, our school stood as more than a center of learning—it was a sanctuary. A stronghold where our culture was affirmed, our history taught with pride, and our aspirations nurtured in quiet defiance of the racist America that surrounded us.

Our teachers—many of whom had been shaped by the legacies of slavery, sharecropping, and southern resistance—refused to let our education be dictated by whitewashed textbooks. They taught us what the curriculum omitted: the truth of our heritage, the brilliance of our people, the resistance in our bloodlines. Their lessons planted seeds of pride and power, urging us to question what we were told, to honor who we were, and to walk with purpose, even when the road felt narrow and steep.

Leadership, too, reflected this era of transformation. In June 1964, after more than three decades of service, Dr. George W. Watkins and Mrs. Thelma Watkins retired—icons whose dedication shaped generations. Their departure marked the end of an era and the promise of renewal, as Mr. Todd Dillard briefly stepped in with youthful energy before moving on to a federal career. His successor, Mr. Wilbur Taylor—our former guidance counselor—brought a familiar presence and steady hand to lead us forward. These transitions mirrored our own growth, reminding us that change, though uncomfortable, often signals expansion.

Among the educators who shaped me, one moment stands out: Mrs. Edith Harris, my eighth-grade homeroom teacher. A proud Hampton University graduate and the wife of a Baptist preacher, she carried herself with grace and unshakable dignity. One day, a disruptive student dared to disrespect her. Without raising her voice, she declared, "You need to learn RESPECT. Respect will take you further than anything else in this world." At thirteen, I couldn't yet grasp the full weight of her words. But over time, their wisdom deepened. Respect, I came to understand, was the bedrock of resilience.

High school was not merely an academic experience—it was an emotional crucible. The familiar rhythm of single classrooms gave way to a rotating schedule of specialized courses and new mentors. Mrs. Natalie Boykins taught us Civics and Social Studies with nuance. Miss Mary Hawkins, until her graceful retirement, brought clarity to Algebra and Geometry—roles later carried by Mr. James Moore. Mr. James Coleman wove together the logic of math and the wonder of science, while Rev. C.J. Washington and Mrs. Irene Watkins poured their passion into English. Rev. Guy Boykins made history pulse with meaning, and Mr. Howard Ormond and Mrs. Delores Tupponce taught us not just physical strength, but resilience. From biology with Mrs. Thelma Anderson to foreign languages with Mr. John Puryear, our world widened with every lesson. And through Home Economics, Agriculture, Business, Music, and the arts, teachers like Ms. Bernetha Batts, Mr. Franklin Gilyard, Ms. Edith Jackson, and Mr. Harold Davis cultivated our character and our craft.

These teachers were more than educators—they were architects of possibility. They guided us through clubs, councils, and competitions:

Future Homemakers and Farmers of America, Student Council, Honor Society, Science Club, the Literary and Dramatics Club. They coached us on basketball courts, conducted our choir rehearsals, and stood in our corners when the world threatened to knock us down.

Still, beneath the surface of those school years, my personal struggles simmered. As my body changed and my interest in boys grew, so did my self-doubt. I became preoccupied with my appearance, comparing myself endlessly, aching for reassurance I never received. At home, these feelings found no sanctuary. My mother, bound by generational silence, didn't speak of body image, heartbreak, or the invisible wounds girls often carry. And in our community, girls who spoke of unwanted touch were dismissed, labeled "frisky," as though their pain was a character flaw rather than a cry for protection.

That silence was its own kind of violence. My grades slipped. My spirit dimmed. While classmates threw themselves into activities and social events, I stood on the periphery—known for my curious mind, but invisible in the festive rhythm of teenage life. Aside from a brief stint in the Guidance Club and senior year Yearbook Committee, I remained a quiet observer.

And yet, beneath that stillness, something stirred. A quiet resistance. A will to survive. A seed of selfhood that refused to be buried. Even as I floundered, even as I felt unseen, I was becoming. I was learning that endurance is its own kind of triumph.

High school, for all its heartbreak and hardship, taught me to value the quiet victories. It taught me that growth often happens in the shadows— unnoticed, uncelebrated, but no less real. It showed me that survival is sometimes the most radical form of self-love. And that, in a world that sought to silence us, just *being*—whole, questioning, learning—was an act of defiance.

A Class Like No Other: The Unbreakable Spirit of 1969

By the time we stood on the threshold of graduation on June 5, 1969, our modest class of thirty had forged something far deeper than friendship. We were bound by years of shared triumphs, silent struggles, and the unspoken understanding that we were part of something greater—a legacy of perseverance and purpose. Over the decades, that bond has endured, stretching across time, unbreakable even as life carried us down different paths.

Each day within those hallowed halls, I navigated the delicate balance between external expectations and my own internal battles. High school was more than an academic checkpoint—it was the heartbeat of a changing society, a bridge between the comfort of the familiar and the uncertainty of the future. The fiery passion of our teachers, the rhythm of our vibrant clubs, and the quiet defiance of those who challenged racial boundaries lit something within me—a gentle but insistent revolution. A reckoning. A call to find my voice in a world being reborn.

Those years became a crucible in which education intertwined with life's deepest lessons. Leadership transitions, the push for integration, and personal trials collided to shape an era that demanded courage and clarity. I wrestled with questions of identity, self-worth, and whether I was meant to walk a path carved by others or to carve one of my own. The questions came in waves, unsettling and persistent—Was I only what others expected me to be? Could I become something more?

And yet, even in my moments of doubt, there was light. There was fire. There was hope that flickered, even when it faltered. In looking back, I don't only see the confusion and ache of adolescence—I see the stirrings of something sacred: a hunger for justice, the rise of resilience, and the wisdom that blooms in both solitude and solidarity.

George W. Watkins High School became the vessel for my awakening. Surrounded by the echoes of those who had paved the way before me and guided by the steady hands of our elders, I began to see that education was never meant to be passive. It wasn't just something to receive—it was something to claim. With every spirited classroom debate, every late night spent buried in books, and every stolen moment of reflection, I discovered that the true gift of education is self-determination.

I learned a vital truth: when education is anchored in one's cultural heritage, it becomes an unstoppable force for transformation. It gave me permission to think independently, to stand firm in my convictions— even when those convictions challenged the status quo. My years at George Watkins instilled in me the belief that learning is not a destination, but a lifelong dialogue—a sacred conversation between the past and the possible.

Now, looking back through the lens of time, I see that my high school years were never confined to textbooks or exams. They were chapters in a larger narrative—one of resilience, of pride, and of the enduring power of respect. Those formative years built the foundation of my being, cultivating in me a devotion to truth, a reverence for heritage, and the courage to chart my own divine course.

As I continue this journey, I carry with me every lesson etched into those pivotal years: the delicate dance between tradition and transformation, the strength of mentorship, and the unrelenting pursuit of a knowledge that doesn't just inform—but liberates. The world will continue to change, as it always has. But one truth remains steadfast: the path we choose is our own, and within that choice lies the most powerful transformation of all.

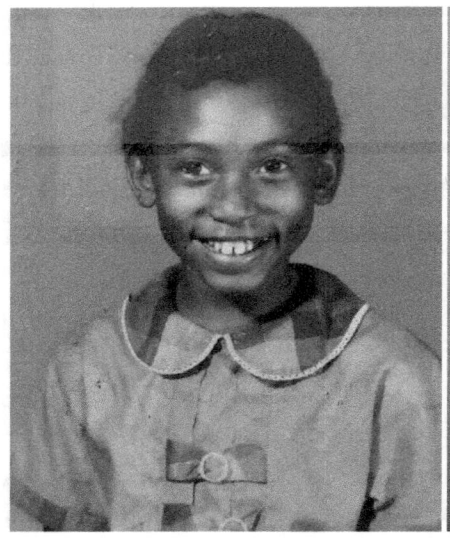
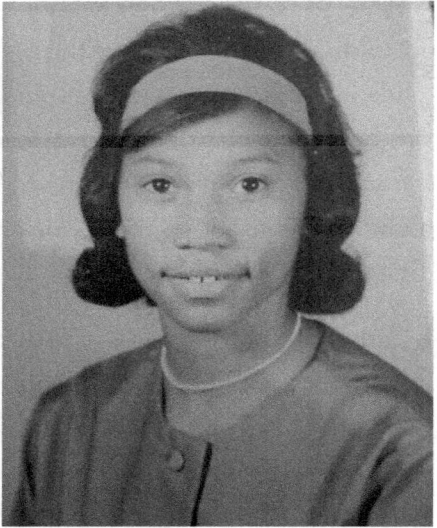

Gwen (2nd Grade)   Gwen (7th grade)

Larry's Graduation   Gwen's Graduation Picture

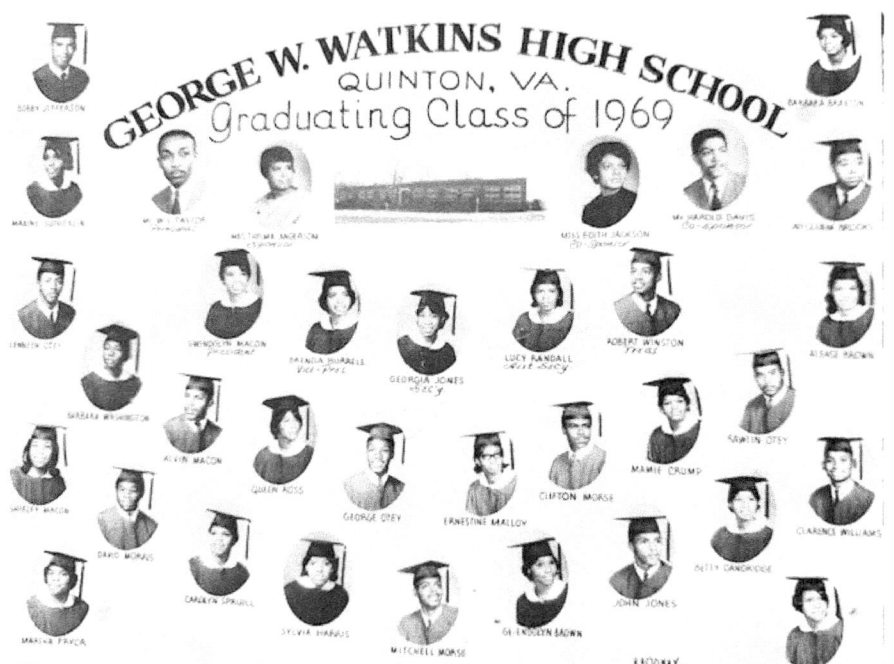

Gwen's Graduating Class

CHAPTER 6

NAVIGATING THE UNCHARTED WATERS OF INDEPENDENCE AND RESPONSIBILITY

Turning the Page, Embracing a New Chapter

After an eventful summer shaped by unexpected lessons and silent revelations, I stood on the cusp of something new—both hesitant and hopeful. In late August of 1969, my bags packed with equal parts fear and expectation, I prepared to leave home for Virginia State College in Petersburg. With suitcases loaded and my heart heavy with uncertainty, Mommy, Daddy, Pinkie, and I climbed into Daddy's maroon 1964 Chevrolet and pulled out onto the open road.

Even now, it's difficult to fully describe the swirl of emotions that overtook me during that drive. I often wondered what thoughts crossed Mommy and Daddy's minds as they prepared to release their daughter into a world far beyond their reach. They had always been protective—especially Mommy, whose careful vigilance often bordered on smothering. And Pinkie, who had been entrusted to my care since she came to live with us at age six, wore her pride and sorrow like twin veils as she sat beside me in the back seat.

As we drove along Route 1 through Colonial Heights—the gateway to the VSC campus—Daddy's voice broke the quiet with a somber warning:

> "Colored people have to be very careful coming through this place. The police here are racist. They'll lock you up for no reason."

His words hung in the air like a low fog, heavy and unshakable. Pinkie and I exchanged a glance but said nothing. We turned our eyes to the passing scenery, each lost in a quiet reckoning about what the future might demand of us.

Then, suddenly, we arrived. The campus buzzed with motion—cars lining the dormitories, parents embracing their children in teary farewells. I was assigned to Byrd Hall, the girls' dormitory, and though I tried to hold my head high, my heart quivered with both anticipation and fear. A flicker of relief passed through my parents when Daddy spotted a familiar couple, Courtney and Mary Brown, who were dropping off their daughter Linda, another freshman. That brief, familiar connection gave them comfort. I was not entirely alone here.

Soon, the moment came. We exchanged goodbyes—tight hugs, trembling smiles—and then they were gone. I stood on the steps of Byrd Hall, the door to a new chapter wide open before me. As their car disappeared down the road, tears blurred my view. A lump settled in my throat. Could I do this? Was I smart enough? Strong enough? Had I been prepared for the demands of this new world?

Room 310 waited for me on the third floor. Inside, I met my roommate, Wanda Randleman from Richmond. Her life seemed like something out of a novel—raised by two elderly aunts, both retired teachers and former socialites, she carried herself with a kind of polished grace that felt both foreign and fascinating to me. Across the hall lived Carolyn Eggleston from Farmville. Her family owned the Eggleston Funeral

Home, and though quiet at first, she exuded a quiet confidence that hinted at strong roots.

Together, we formed a triangle of contrasts—different backgrounds, different lives—but all poised at the starting line of something that would shape us deeply.

Weathering a Year of Change

My freshman year at Virginia State College was a storm of contradictions—possibility met with self-doubt, promise weighed down by insecurity. As I walked the halls of VSC, I realized I had stepped into a world both vibrant and unfamiliar, where students arrived from every corner of the country, carrying with them the polish of preparation I didn't possess. Many were children of VSC alumni—doctors, lawyers, educators, business owners. Their families had paved their way with firsthand experience, advice, and confidence.

I, on the other hand, often felt adrift. My father had only a third-grade education; my mother, a seventh. Their lives were spent in labor—cleaning houses, chauffeuring for affluent white families, cooking in diners, working in tobacco factories. Daddy had just retired from the American Tobacco Company. Mommy still worked long hours as a cook and waitress at Hechler's Restaurant in Richmond. Every penny they saved was a sacrifice, a testament to their dream that I would have a better life than they had ever imagined for themselves.

They gave everything—quietly, consistently—for me. Their love was measured in worn shoes, tip jars, packed lunches, and stretched budgets. And still, as I tried to find my footing on campus, I struggled to believe I belonged.

From the very beginning, it felt like the odds were stacked against me. I scored poorly on placement tests and was placed in remedial math and English. I wasn't athletic or outgoing, nor did I find comfort in the rowdy card games that echoed through the dorm halls at night. I didn't sing, couldn't dance, and lacked the rhythm and boldness that others wore so easily. Instead, I stayed in my dorm room, quietly overwhelmed, too ashamed to ask how to play spades or bid whist, watching from behind a veil of longing.

Every weekend, I returned home. Partly because I missed the familiarity of family, and partly because of Arthur. He was four years older, already finished with a two-year degree in electronics from Norfolk State, and my parents regarded him as a steady, responsible presence. They hoped he would be a stabilizing force in my life, someone to help steer me away from the difficulties that had shaped my birthmother's journey.

But even Arthur couldn't anchor me during that turbulent year. My father's health began to deteriorate. A lifetime of chain smoking caught up with him. His weight dropped, his eyes dulled, and he began experiencing troubling urinary symptoms. I worried deeply. One day, Carolyn—my dorm neighbor—noticed my concern and gently offered insight.

> "Gwen," she said, 'get your father to the doctor. He's probably diabetic. My father went into a diabetic coma. I recognize the signs".

Her words hit hard. I begged Daddy to get checked, but he refused. Desperate, I called Aunt Evelyn in Philadelphia, hoping she could convince him. She did. And Carolyn was right—Daddy was diagnosed with diabetes. Thankfully, with medication, his condition improved. But the emotional toll—the fear, the helplessness—pulled my focus from school. My grades plummeted. By the end of the year, I was on academic probation with a GPA just above 1.0.

With Daddy's health and my academic struggles weighing me down, I made a difficult decision: I wouldn't return for my sophomore year. I couldn't bear to watch my parents continue sacrificing while I was barely staying afloat.

I felt lost. Confused. Unsure of who I was or what I truly wanted. Part of me wondered if marriage could be the answer. Could it offer the stability I longed for? Could it help me rewrite the narrative of my family—one marked by generations of women raising children alone?

My grandmother had never married. My birthmother hadn't either. Nor had four of my maternal great-aunts. They all bore children, but carried the heavy burdens of raising them alone. Their lives were full of love but also hardship, and I wanted something different. Perhaps what I really yearned for was the bond I saw between Mommy and Daddy— partnership, protection, shared purpose. I wanted to be loved that way.

After leaving college, I took a job as a clerk at the Division of Motor Vehicles in Richmond. I lived at home at first, but eventually, restlessness crept in. I craved freedom—true independence.

I liked the work. I liked the space. But Arthur remained a constant presence. Persistent and determined, he pursued me earnestly, making it hard for me to meet anyone else or explore other paths. At the time, dating more than one person was frowned upon. A young woman's reputation was fragile, and I felt the pressure to settle down, to conform to expectations before I even knew who I was becoming.

Living at home meant comfort, but it also came with limits. I couldn't fully explore my identity. I couldn't spread my wings. Marriage began to feel like the clearest way to claim a life of my own, a door to independence rather than a cage.

Arthur proposed on December 25, 1970. We set our wedding date for May 15, 1971.

I accepted with equal parts hope and hesitation. Was this love? Or was it an exit strategy? Was I stepping into something sacred, or simply reaching for the next rung on the ladder out of uncertainty?

I didn't know the answers then. But I knew I was standing on the edge of something life-changing.

MY JOURNEY THROUGH PAIN AND GROWTH

Expectations Shattered

As the wedding date approached, a quiet but relentless anxiety took hold of me—pressing on my mind, body, and soul. Beneath the surface, I felt the unmistakable tug of misalignment, a deep sense that this path was not one divinely designed for me. Still, I continued forward—not out of conviction, but out of fear. I didn't want to disappoint my parents, whose sacrifices and expectations weighed heavily on my heart.

Looking back, the red flags were bold and waving, but I told myself they could be folded away with patience and love. I believed I could mold the man I was marrying, soften his edges, and help him grow. I convinced myself that with time and effort, things would change. I also convinced myself that calling off the wedding—so close to the big day—would bring unbearable shame and disappointment.

From the beginning, Arthur and I were unequally yoked. He was the oldest of three children, raised by a single mother who had endured much to provide for her family. When I asked about his father, Arthur lied, claiming he had passed away. The truth eventually surfaced during a casual conversation with his mother—a revelation that shook my trust and deepened the cracks already forming.

Arthur often made himself the center of every moment. His needs, his stories, his presence overshadowed everything else. I found myself constantly trying to soothe his ego, accommodate his moods, and ignore the subtle but steady erosion of my own confidence. I didn't understand then how deeply self-centeredness could poison a marriage. I only knew that I felt myself dimming.

Despite the unease growing inside me, I moved forward. On May 15, 1971, surrounded by smiling faces and shimmering expectations, I walked down the aisle. My father stood beside me in his tuxedo, beaming with pride. I wore a flowing white gown, its train trailing behind me like the dreams I was trying to believe in. The church was filled with family and friends. To them, it was a picture-perfect moment. But inside, I was unraveling.

With each step toward the altar, I heard a voice—a soft, persistent whisper from deep within:

You still have time to turn back. You don't have to do this.

It was the voice of my spirit, pleading with me to listen. But another voice, louder and laced with duty and social pressure, replied:

It's too late now. You'll be okay.

My heart was in turmoil. My father's steady arm held mine, but my mind was adrift—torn between choosing freedom and preserving appearances. I had silenced my intuition for too long. The signs had been there, but fear had kept me walking.

As the vows were spoken, I felt both present and absent, standing at the intersection of hope and hesitation. My spirit cried for release, but my feet kept moving, ushered by tradition, obedience, and the ache to make things right—even when they weren't.

Beyond the Vows: The Journey Begins

At just 20 years old, I was stepping into a life I wasn't fully prepared for. After a small reception at my parents' home, Arthur and I were supposed to begin our life together in Chesapeake, Virginia. But before we could leave, his mother made an unexpected request: she insisted he take her home to Gloucester—on our wedding day. Every other ride had been declined.

I sat in stunned silence as we detoured through Gloucester before continuing to Chesapeake. It was a symbolic beginning—one that hinted at the detours, imbalances, and unexpected obligations that would define much of our relationship.

Arthur worked at the Norfolk Naval Base, and after a few months, I began searching for work. I was eventually hired as a sales associate at Penney's Department Store, which later led to a clerk position at Travelers Insurance Company. Though I was grateful for the income, something inside me stirred—I wanted more. I missed learning. I missed the challenge of education.

So I enrolled at Norfolk State University and registered for a sociology class titled *Social Problems* taught by Dr. Joseph Samuels. I poured my energy into a research paper on venereal diseases, a timely and serious public health issue. When I received the paper back, a bold A+ adorned the top—but more impactful than the grade was the handwritten note:

"Please see me."

With nervous curiosity, I met with Dr. Samuels. To my surprise, he offered high praise for my research and writing. At that moment, something shifted. For the first time in a long time, I saw myself through a different lens—capable, intelligent, worthy. His affirmation planted a seed of confidence that would later blossom into my love for research and writing.

As I settled into life in Chesapeake, friendships began to form. Through work and Arthur's social circles, I met kind and welcoming people. Many of Arthur's childhood friends had also moved to the Tidewater area with their wives, forming a small but vibrant community. Donald "Duck" Larrimore and his wife Mabel lived nearby, as did George and Virginia Evans, and George and Patricia Wake. As young parents, we bonded over the chaos of child-rearing, often gathering for playdates, backyard barbecues, or pick-up basketball games.

Weekends were often spent back home with family or visiting close friends. One of my favorite memories was visiting the home of Mr. and Mrs. Herman and Earlene Booker. Their home was more than a house—it was a sanctuary. Mrs. Booker, treated every guest like royalty. Her dining table was always set with fine china and polished silver. She had spent her career working as a cook and housekeeper for wealthy white families, but in her own home, she extended nothing but dignity, warmth, and culinary brilliance.

Her meals were legendary—roast beef, turkey, lamb chops, pork loin— all seasoned to perfection and served with elegance. Her motto said it all:

"If they eat well, my children and family will eat well too."

In the heart of that warm, bustling kitchen, I saw an example of grace, pride, and legacy. It reminded me that even amid the uncertainty of my new marriage and shifting dreams, there were still spaces where I could feel nourished, seen, and inspired.

A New Life Amidst Uncertainty

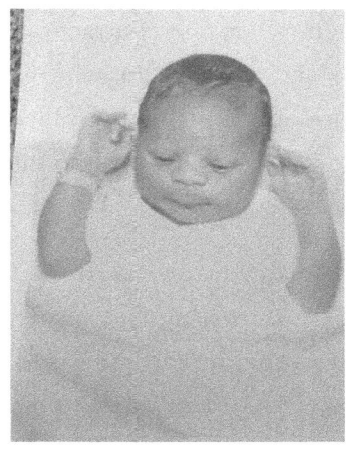

Arthur LeDon Thornton

As time moved forward and I adjusted to the rhythms of married life, we were met with heartbreaking news in 1972: Papa had fallen seriously ill. He was hospitalized and later diagnosed with cancer. We watched helplessly as his once-vigorous frame weakened, his strength slipping away, and his presence becoming quieter and more fragile with each passing day.

Meanwhile, my marriage to Arthur was already showing signs of strain. We faced ongoing challenges that left me questioning whether starting a family was the right decision. And yet, in early February 1973, I learned I was pregnant.

When I shared the news with Arthur, I hoped—desperately—for excitement, for even a flicker of joy that might soften the tension between us. Instead, his reaction was flat, distant. The support and concern I craved were nowhere to be found. As my body underwent profound changes and my emotions swelled with both anticipation and fear, his self-absorbed behavior only grew more pronounced. I was forced to walk this path largely alone.

With much prayer, I endured. I chose not to burden my parents with the full weight of my struggles, especially not Daddy, whose health was now in decline. I later learned he had his own quiet reservations about Arthur but kept them to himself, believing silence was a form of protection for his "princess."

The experience of labor and childbirth would prove to be one of the most physically and emotionally grueling moments of my life.

It was Sunday, November 4th, mid-afternoon, when the contractions began. I told Arthur, hoping for tenderness and support. Instead, he responded with indifference, offering no comfort or urgency. I called my doctor, who advised me to monitor my contractions and head to the hospital when they reached five-minute intervals.

Hours passed. The pain intensified. Arthur remained disengaged. As I twisted and turned in agony, he took his time showering and moved with maddening slowness, as though he had all the time in the world. Finally, around 11 p.m., he drove me—leisurely—to DePaul Hospital in Norfolk, Virginia, ignoring my pleas to hurry.

Once admitted, the night stretched endlessly. My son seemed in no rush to arrive. I begged for a C-section, but the medical team assured me I could deliver naturally. Hours passed. Exhaustion consumed me. At last, x-rays revealed what I had long suspected—my baby was not properly positioned for birth.

Eventually, I was given an epidural. It numbed me just in time. By the time the anesthesia took effect, I was barely conscious.

Adding insult to injury, Arthur left the hospital—telling the staff he was going home to rest. He didn't return until the next day, after our son had already been born.

Arthur "LeDon" Thornton entered the world on November 6, 1973, at 5:21 a.m.—a healthy 8 lbs. 4 oz., and 21 inches long. Due to the complications of my delivery, I developed a fever and was unable to hold or breastfeed him right away. It broke my heart to miss that sacred first moment of bonding. It felt like one more loss in a series of sacrifices that had brought me to this point.

Ironically, my due date had been in late October, but my son—like so much in my life at that time—arrived on his own terms.

That very morning, Papa was scheduled for surgery. My mother, his devoted caregiver, was caught in a painful dilemma—torn between being at his side or traveling to Chesapeake to be with me. She chose to remain with him, trusting she could come once the baby was born.

Anointed in Love: Christening of My Precious Child

5 Generation:
Coreine, Mary Frances, Gwen, Papa, LeDon

The moment I cradled my newborn son against my heart, I knew—without question—that he was a divine gift. The pain of labor dissolved instantly, eclipsed by an overwhelming sense of gratitude and awe. In my arms lay the firstborn of the fifth generation in the Ida and William A. Christian family line—a new link in a cherished, living legacy.

Fate had braided our story in such a remarkable way: my grandmother, Coreine, was the eldest of their ten living children; her daughter, Mary Frances, was the first grandchild; I held the honor of being the first great-grandchild; and now, my son was the newest branch—another chapter in a sacred generational journey.

In the weeks and months that followed, my heart overflowed with a depth of love I had never known. Words could scarcely contain my gratitude for the life entrusted to me. And so, with reverence and joy, we planned a dedication service—an intimate offering to return this precious child to the One who gave him, to anoint him with divine blessing, and to surround him with the grace and protection of our faith.

Despite still recovering from surgery, Papa's desire to be present for the christening of his great-great-grandson was unshakable. With quiet resolve, he summoned the strength to join us on Sunday, January 13, 1974. Watching him bear witness to that sacred moment felt like the closing of one chapter and the beginning of another. As my son was blessed, I felt it deeply in my spirit: he belonged to God. And with that knowledge came peace—no harm, no hardship, no shadow would ever be greater than the divine covering that now rested over him.

Nearly four months later, on May 2, 1974, Papa made his final transition. He left this world as he had lived in it—with dignity, faith, and unwavering love. His legacy lives on in every heartbeat of our family, in every prayer spoken over the generations he helped raise, and in the enduring resilience he modeled until the very end.

A Bold New Direction

In the summer of 1974, with a wife and an eight-month-old son, Arthur made the decision to join the U.S. Army. As he embarked on his military journey, I returned to my parents' home, where my son and I stayed for about a year and a half. By 1976, I secured a job as a dental assistant and receptionist —determined to create stability for myself and my child.

During this period, my parents gifted me an acre of land to build a home. Unaware of the growing turmoil in my marriage, they deeded the land in both our names. Together, Arthur and I built a modest three-bedroom Jim Walter home. It cost just $22,000—but the emotional cost of our relationship was immeasurable.

Arthur's military assignments took him to Georgia and later to Alaska, but distance did nothing to soften the challenges between us. His behavior became increasingly controlling, his words sharp and cruel, and eventually, his threats turned physical. When he crossed that line, I knew I had to protect myself and my son. Emotionally depleted and mentally worn, I made the difficult but necessary decision to file for divorce.

At twenty-five, I found myself a young mother facing an uncertain future—but beneath the fear, there was a quiet strength that refused to be extinguished. Then, in what felt like a divinely orchestrated moment, a patient named Shirley Goodall walked into the dental office. We struck up a conversation, and I confided in her my desire to return to school. Her response was simple, yet life-altering:

"Have you ever thought about social work?"

Without hesitation, I said, "Yes. That's what I've always wanted to do."

Encouraged by her words, I reached out to Virginia Commonwealth University (VCU) and scheduled an appointment with Dr. David Beverly, Director of the BSW Program. When the day arrived, I stepped into his office with a mix of nervousness and anticipation. Dr. Beverly, tall and soft-spoken with snow-white hair, welcomed me with quiet kindness. He asked me to share my story—and I did. He listened intently. When I finished, he looked at me and simply said:

"I will give you a chance."

Those six words ignited a fire in me. They were the spark I needed to step boldly into the future I had long dreamed of.

Finding Strength and Solace in Therapy

In the fall of 1976, I began my journey as a part-time student at Virginia Commonwealth University, finally pursuing my dream of becoming a social worker. My first course—**Introduction to Social Work** with Professor Jane Reeves—confirmed what I had always known: this was my calling. I earned an "A," and in that moment, my confidence began to bloom.

At the time, I was still working as a receptionist at Dr. McCain's dental office, helping build his success while quietly longing to build my own. With my parents graciously providing childcare, I found the courage to balance work, school, and motherhood—despite the weight of exhaustion and financial strain.

Arthur, meanwhile, offered no emotional or financial support. His sharp words were designed to diminish:

"You'll never make it without me."

But his cruelty became my fuel. I was determined to prove him wrong— and to prove to myself that I could build a future rooted in independence and purpose.

The pressure of juggling so many responsibilities began to take its toll. I found comfort in blues legends like B.B. King, Bobby "Blue" Bland, and Etta James—voices that gave melody to my silent sorrow. One day, a kind and observant patient, Ms. Ethel Daniels, noticed the sadness in my eyes and gently encouraged me to seek help.

"Call Dr. Charles Christian," she said. **"He's the only Black psychiatrist in Richmond."**

I took her advice.

Dr. Christian was a man of extraordinary depth. Born and raised in Charles City County, Virginia, he graduated from Ruthville High School and later Virginia State College before earning his medical degree in psychiatry from the Medical College of Virginia. He served in Vietnam, where exposure to Agent Orange eventually led to his diagnosis of Parkinson's disease. Upon returning home, he opened a private practice in Richmond and became a pioneer—breaking barriers in a field few African Americans had yet entered.

His approach to therapy was client-centered, solution-focused, and grounded in a strength perspective. He saw his patients fully—culturally, spiritually, and emotionally—and offered them a space where their pain was not minimized but honored.

After weeks of hesitation, I finally picked up the phone—and to my surprise, he answered personally. That call changed the trajectory of my life.

At our first session, I was trembling. He greeted me with warmth and invited me into his office, a space filled with green plants, thoughtful artwork, and two plush recliners. He allowed me time to settle, then gently asked,

"What brings you to see me today?"

I began to speak—about my broken marriage, my fears, my pain—but tried to do so with composure. When he noticed me fighting back tears, he said,

"You're trying to be Superwoman, aren't you?"

And with that, my walls collapsed. I cried—deep, guttural sobs that released years of silent suffering. It was the first time I understood: I didn't have to carry it all alone.

Just two months into therapy, tragedy struck. On **January 29, 1977**, my beloved cousin, Jean DePriest Otey, took her own life and that of her four-year-old son, Tiger (Ulysees, Jr.). She had been battling deep depression and the collapse of her marriage. The shock shattered me. My own marriage was unraveling. My son was the same age as Tiger. I descended into despair.

One night, overwhelmed by grief, I sat on the edge of my bed and held a pistol in my hand. I was ready to end the pain. But then, I heard the voice of my great-grandmother:

"Precious child, take my hand."

That whisper saved me.

I put the gun down and lay back on my bed. What followed was an out-of-body experience—a descent into a dark tunnel, where no light shone, yet I felt enveloped by peace.

In my soul, I whispered, **"If I'm dead, let me stay dead."**

But a voice responded:

"I'm not finished with you yet. I have something else for you to do."

When I awoke, I knew my life had been spared for a purpose. I never again entertained thoughts of ending it.

Later, in therapy, I confessed to Dr. Christian that I wasn't sure if I still believed in God. He looked at me with gentle wisdom and said,

"Gwen, you must believe in something—even if it's no more than that chair sitting in the corner."

His words were simple, but profound. They gave me space to rebuild my faith slowly, authentically.

For twelve years, Dr. Christian was my anchor—the one person I could trust completely. He guided me with patience, empathy, and unwavering care. I know without question: he was sent by God. A healer. A helper. An angel whose presence lit the darkest parts of my journey.

Embracing a Path Free from the Past
In Pursuit: My Higher Educational Journey

With Dr. Christian's unwavering support and wisdom, I began the courageous work of reclaiming my own story—no longer bound by a script written by fear, tradition, or the expectations of others. My faith blossomed in this season of renewal, and my connection to a Higher Power became a steady compass guiding me forward.

In 1978, I made a daring and life-changing decision. I resigned from my full-time job at the dentist's office, stepped out on faith, and enrolled full-time in Virginia Commonwealth University's Bachelor of Social Work program. It was a leap into the unknown—frightening, yes, but fueled by a calling I could no longer ignore.

To support myself and my son, I cobbled together a path of survival and sacrifice. I qualified for financial aid, applied for food stamp assistance, and worked two part-time jobs—all while carrying a full academic load of 18 credit hours. It was an exhausting rhythm, but purpose made it bearable.

As I pursued my studies, my faith deepened. Seeking a richer understanding of my spiritual path, I took an elective course on religion. That class opened my eyes to the many ways people connect to the Divine—how belief becomes not only a source of inner peace but a wellspring of strength in the face of adversity.

Before leaving the dental office, I had formed a friendship with a kind and compassionate man named Patrick "Pat" Brown. Even after I resigned, he remained present in my life—not romantically at first, but as a steady, respectful friend who offered encouragement, care, and material support. Over time, our bond matured into something sacred.

Pat stood by me when times were lean. He made sure my son and I never went without, forming a sincere connection not only with me but also with my parents—especially my father, with whom he shared a quiet mutual respect.

He became my anchor during one of the stormiest chapters of my life, embodying the strength of my earthly father and the mercy of my Heavenly One. One of the most memorable gestures he made was surprising me with a celebratory trip to Atlanta, Georgia, after I received my final divorce decree. It was my first time on an airplane, and from the moment we touched down, he treated me like royalty—elevating my spirit and affirming my worth at a time when I needed it most.

Pat's selfless love and steady friendship were nothing short of divine intervention. In a season marked by uncertainty, he was another angel placed on my path—there not to rescue me, but to remind me I was worthy of joy, dignity, and peace.

In May 1980, at just twenty-nine years old, I stood in cap and gown and crossed the stage to receive my Bachelor of Social Work degree from Virginia Commonwealth University. That moment felt like standing inside a dream—a reality shaped by prayer, perseverance, and the relentless belief that better was possible.

I scanned the crowd and saw my parents, beaming with pride. The joy in their eyes spoke volumes—of every sacrifice they had made, every burden they had quietly borne to help me reach that day. This milestone was not mine alone; it belonged to all of us.

It was God's grace, my parents' love, and the timely presence of earthly angels that carried me through. I had endured sleepless nights, emotional exhaustion, and moments of deep doubt. But I rose—again and again—driven by faith and a fire that would not be extinguished.

Still, I wasn't done.

Fueled by the momentum of achievement, I immediately applied to VCU's Master of Social Work Advanced Standing Program. When my acceptance letter arrived, I felt a holy confirmation that I was, indeed, walking in purpose.

One year later, in May 1981, I stood once again in celebration—this time holding a master's degree in my hands. It was more than an academic victory. It was proof that faith, work, and courage can transform a broken beginning into a triumphant legacy.

Through every challenge, I had discovered strength. In every season of doubt, I found faith. My path had never been easy—but it had always, unquestionably, been worth it.

Challenges, Purpose, and Triumphs

When I graduated from VCU, I still owed approximately $900 in tuition. Yet, by the grace of God, I walked across that stage, diploma in hand. As I stood there, the weight of accomplishment mingled with uncertainty. *Now what?* I wondered. *Where do I go from here?*

In the 1970s and 1980s, a troubling disparity defined the adoption landscape. The demand for healthy white infants far exceeded the number available, while countless Black children remained in foster care—waiting, often indefinitely, for permanent, loving homes. At the same time, few Black families were actively seeking adoption, a gap compounded by the lack of Black social workers in the field.

In 1972, the National Association of Black Social Workers issued a powerful statement opposing the placement of Black children in white homes, emphasizing the necessity of preserving cultural identity, community roots, and psychological well-being. In response, the Children's Home Society of Virginia (CHS) began actively recruiting Black professionals to help place Black children with Black families.

That's where I came in.

Immediately after earning my degree, I was hired by CHS. It was a deeply personal mission for me. As an adopted child myself, I understood both the challenges and the transformative power of belonging. I knew firsthand the importance of keeping children connected to their heritage, and I was committed to being part of that change.

During my time at CHS, I successfully recruited numerous African American families to adopt Black children. I participated in media campaigns, led community workshops, and co-founded the Richmond Black Adoption Organization. One of my proudest accomplishments was helping bring Father George Clements to Richmond—a Catholic priest and civil rights activist who had marched with Dr. Martin Luther King Jr.

In 1980, Father Clements launched the national One-Church, One-Child Program to encourage every Black church to adopt one Black child in need. After receiving special approval from the Vatican, he adopted the first of four children in 1981 and traveled the country, urging others to do the same. His mission inspired a cultural shift and brought new visibility to the needs of Black children in foster care.

Through this work, I met extraordinary people—hopeful parents, passionate advocates, and tireless community leaders all working to reimagine what family could look like for vulnerable youth. The impact was powerful, but the road was not without its burdens.

Despite my professional achievements, personal trials loomed large. While I was pursuing my education and beginning my career, my ex-husband continued to harass me, refusing to pay child support and disrupting my peace at every opportunity. I later learned, through his cousin-in-law Polly, that he had remarried less than a month after our divorce. As if that betrayal weren't enough, he began seeking legal custody of our son and even received military orders to Germany—likely an attempt to evade his financial obligations through international relocation.

The stress was unbearable. I spiraled into a deep depression, gripped by the fear of losing my child and overwhelmed by emotional exhaustion. During those harrowing days, Dr. Christian remained a constant source of strength and grounding. His guidance was life-saving.

And yet, God continued to send helpers along the way.

While working at CHS, I met Dr. Michelle Whitehurst-Cook and her husband, Lee. Our connection was instant. At the time, she was completing her residency at Riverside Hospital in Newport News. When she later accepted a position as a family doctor in Providence Forge—just a few miles from my parents' home—I knew her presence in my life was more than coincidence. It was divine placement.

Dr. Whitehurst-Cook was born and raised in Lawrenceville, Virginia, in a home where education and service were core values. Her father, a biology professor at St. Paul's College—an HBCU in Brunswick County—had shaped generations of young minds. Her mother was equally committed to nurturing the community, working as an elementary school teacher and guiding children in their earliest years.

Following in their footsteps, Dr. Whitehurst-Cook graduated from the College of William & Mary and went on to earn her medical degree from the Medical College of Virginia. She specialized in rural health, a field that reflected her passion for serving the underserved and extending quality care to forgotten corners of the Commonwealth.

Through every step of her career, she honored her parents' legacy—blending academic excellence with community care. Her journey was a shining example of purpose, discipline, and heart.

Alongside Dr. Farrar Howard, Michelle and Lee became cherished members of my support system. They were not just friends—they were family, walking beside me during one of the most vulnerable seasons of my life.

LeDon & Pat

Lee & Michelle Cook

CHAPTER 9

PAIN, PERSEVERANCE, AND STRENGTH

Loss, Struggles, and Unwavering Love

As I look back on the 1980s, I know—without a doubt—it was only by the grace of God and the guiding hands of my ancestors that I made it through each trial and tribulation.

On December 5, 1981, tragedy struck our family again. Uncle Harold—Mommy and her sisters' only brother—went deer hunting early that cold Saturday morning with Mr. Moses Friday and several others. Not long after entering the woods, we received a devastating call: Uncle Harold had died suddenly.

The following year, 1982, was consumed by a grueling custody battle with my ex-husband, who relentlessly pursued full custody of our son. At the same time, my friendship with Pat began to fade. Looking back, I realize how deeply my emotional and mental turmoil contributed to that loss. I was overwhelmed—mentally, emotionally, physically, and spiritually.

As the year ended, I felt desperate for a fresh start. On New Year's Eve, Mommy attended the Watch Night service at church, while Daddy came over to sit with me and LeDon and watch the ball drop in Times Square.

There beside us, I saw the concern in his eyes. He was worried—not just for me, but for his little sidekick, LeDon—as the looming custody battle cast its shadow over us.

I thought things couldn't possibly get worse. I was wrong.

On February 11, 1983, my life changed forever.

For a week leading up to that day, I had a growing, inescapable sense that death was near. My depression was suffocating. I felt consumed by darkness and told Mommy and Daddy where to find my documents and insurance papers—just in case.

That Friday morning, a fierce snowstorm blanketed the world. As LeDon and I made our way to my parents' house for breakfast, I sat beside the wood stove, my head bowed in sorrow.

Daddy looked at me and said gently, "Baby, it looks like you've lost your last friend."

I sighed, "Maybe I have, Daddy."

Without hesitation, he replied, "No, baby—you got me. I am your friend."

Those words landed like a balm. He had always been my hero—but in that moment, I realized he was my truest friend as well.

Despite the storm, LeDon and I decided to go to the little country store, just two miles away. As we cleared the driveway, Daddy came outside, eager to help. At 78, he struggled to breathe in the bitter cold, and I insisted he return inside. He did—reluctantly.

What should have been a quick trip stretched into two hours through heavy snow. But even through that exhausting journey, Daddy's words stayed with me, warming a heart that had nearly gone numb.

After we returned and shared a few moments at my parents' house, LeDon and I walked home—a short distance, just across the field. The wind had flung our front door wide open, and I immediately called for Daddy's help.

"I'll be right over," he replied.

While I searched for tools, LeDon looked outside and saw him, already at the back door, gasping for air. He made it inside, collapsed into a chair, and asked me to help him take off his boots. I gently removed them and told him to rest.

As he shuffled into the living room, LeDon and I exchanged a worried glance. Then a loud thump shattered the quiet.

"Granddaddy!" LeDon screamed.

I dropped to my knees beside Daddy, trying desperately to revive him—but he was gone. In shock, LeDon ran across the snow-covered field to get Mommy, as the storm had rendered our phone useless.

I raced through the swirling wind to my parents' house, grabbed Mommy's hand, and we returned together. Her cries filled our home as she collapsed beside his still form. LeDon stood quietly, only nine years old, his wide eyes filled with a pain too deep for words.

Aunt Tweedie Weedie and her family, who lived across the field, soon heard the news. We reached out to my dear friend Dr. Michelle Whitehurst-Cook. An alert summoned an EMT from the neighborhood, who arrived quickly and worked valiantly—but it was too late. Dr. Whitehurst-Cook arrived moments later and confirmed what we already knew. My father was gone.

Family and friends gathered as the storm raged on. LeDon and I sat quietly, waiting for the undertaker, our silence heavy with grief.

I remembered a moment from when LeDon was six. We were watching the news with Daddy, and a story about abuse came on. LeDon had asked, "Mommy, what is sex?"

Startled, I answered, "Ask your granddaddy."

Without missing a beat, Daddy replied, "Eating bread before it's cooked."

Now, three years later, sitting beside me after his death, LeDon whispered, "Granddaddy never got a chance to tell me what it means to eat bread before it's cooked."

His words broke me and reminded me: my honesty with him was more than necessary—it was sacred.

Planning Daddy's funeral was excruciating. I involved LeDon in every decision. He chose the shirt and tie he had gifted Daddy for Christmas, and the little shoes Daddy loved. Each detail was a loving tribute from grandson to grandfather.

Weeks later, LeDon turned to me and said, "Mommy, I want to be a funeral director."

I was speechless. "Okay, if that's what you want to do," I managed. But in my heart, I wondered what sorrow had led him to such a choice.

Those months were the darkest of my life. Mommy was inconsolable. LeDon's behavior changed. He grew angry and rebellious. I struggled to hold us all together—emotionally, mentally, spiritually. The custody battle with my ex-husband continued to rage.

We clung to any thread of normalcy. After Daddy's passing, my cousin Jimmy arranged for LeDon to walk to the bus stop with his daughters, Nita and Net, so he wouldn't have to do it alone.

Then, in October, during a routine physical, doctors discovered a nodule in my throat. I needed thyroid surgery. With Mommy caring for LeDon, I faced the hospital alone. The pre-op anxiety and loneliness were crushing. When the IV slid in, I drifted into the deepest sleep I'd known since Daddy's death.

When I woke, my friend Patty Nichols stood beside me, her serene presence like an angel. In her, I saw the reminder that even in the depths of sorrow, God sends light.

Yet guilt consumed me. I questioned whether I had caused Daddy's death by calling him to help that day.

Dr. Christian helped me work through the layers of pain. But I needed spiritual clarity too. I turned to my pastor, Rev. Robert Williams. He listened and then said:

"Sister Gwen, your father was doing what made him happy. He was helping you and his grandson—just as he always had. Maybe, just maybe, it was simply his time. Maybe God led him to your house because your mother wouldn't have survived witnessing his passing."

His words quieted the storm in my heart. Perhaps Daddy's final act— helping us—was not a tragedy, but a testament to his love.

Then something extraordinary happened.

Daddy came to me in three dreams.

In the first, he sat peacefully on his porch under a cloudless sky. The stillness was sacred. He whispered, "Baby, don't worry. I am at peace in the land of the magnificent heavens above."

In the second dream, he entered the kitchen, carrying a bag. Startled, I asked, "Daddy, where have you been? Everybody's been looking for you!"

He replied, "I'm okay. A lot of people I expected to see weren't there." And just like that, he vanished.

Was he telling me he had arrived at his eternal home—where not everyone made it?

In the final dream, my sister and I stood at Union Baptist Church. A strange energy filled the air. A car loomed behind the building, its presence frightening. Suddenly, a figure in white emerged and pointed toward Isgett's Country Store.

It was Daddy.

Without speaking, he told me: I will always be your protector. Your guide. Your light in the dark.

I awoke with tears on my face—but this time, they weren't just tears of sorrow. They were tears of healing.

Daddy was gone, but he was not lost.

He was with me—in the quiet, in the wind, in the whisper of spirit.

He had never really left.

And he never would.

Rebuilding Hearts and Finding Solace

With Daddy gone, life felt like an unfamiliar landscape—one marked by sorrow, uncertainty, and the aching void of his absence. Mommy, then in her late sixties, poured herself into her work as a cook at the Colonial Restaurant in Bottoms Bridge, just two miles from our home. Every morning, long before dawn, she opened the restaurant at 5:00 a.m., brewing coffee, preparing pastries, and crafting hearty Southern breakfasts for early patrons. She was known far and wide for her fried chicken—people came from all over just to get a taste of Miss Alice's finest cooking.

But even the warmth of the kitchen and the rhythm of routine couldn't mask the sadness etched across her face. The year after Daddy's passing, I watched a quiet despair settle into her spirit. She had always been fiercely independent, but Daddy had been her anchor—the wind beneath her wings. Without him, she seemed adrift.

I couldn't stand to see her struggling alone under the weight of grief and responsibility. So, I asked her to move in with me and LeDon. We didn't want her to face the silence of an empty house. She was used to Daddy handling everything—the household repairs, the car maintenance, all the little tasks that had once made life feel steady. Now, every burden felt heavier. Though she tried to press on, I could see her slowly fading beneath the pressure of financial strain and emotional loss.

In our tight-knit village, Mommy wasn't alone in her grief. Other women were walking similar paths, carrying the same sorrow of widowhood. Recognizing their need for connection, I took the initiative to form a support group—a circle of widowed women who could lean on one another and find comfort in community.

Mommy, Mrs. Mary Lou Williams, Mrs. Mary Becoat, Mrs. Madeline Willoughby, Mrs. Catherine Johnson, and Mrs. Henrietta Christian— all had experienced the pain of losing a beloved partner. Together, they began to rediscover joy in each other's company.

We organized outings to breathe life back into our weary spirits. A group cruise aboard the *Spirit of Norfolk* offered a brief escape—an afternoon of music, laughter, and shared memories that softened our grief. We met regularly for lunches and dinners, carving out space for companionship in the midst of sorrow.

Through these gatherings, we came to understand that grief never truly vanishes—it reshapes itself. It settles quietly into the corners of life, showing up in unexpected moments. But in our shared stories, in the gentle understanding of kindred souls, we found glimpses of healing. We rebuilt, slowly, tenderly—one moment of laughter, one act of love at a time.

Strengthening Faith in the Face of Adversity

I continued to pour my heart into my work at the Children's Home Society, giving more than one hundred percent as an adoption worker. Yet beneath the surface, a quiet restlessness stirred—an unease I couldn't quite name, both professionally and personally.

As a single mother, I gave my son everything I had: love, time, and the stability I prayed would carry us through. But as he entered adolescence, that foundation began to tremble. His attitude shifted—resistant, rebellious. I could feel the internal struggle, but I couldn't reach him.

His father remained absent in every way that counted—offering no support, only bitterness that widened the emotional divide. The tension trickled down to our son, rippling in ways I couldn't always see but deeply felt. Soon, the open communication we once shared began to unravel, replaced by silence and emotional distance.

Desperate, I turned to the men in my life—friends, cousins, uncles—searching for guidance I hadn't yet found. Their wisdom helped, but my son remained withdrawn. I sought professional counseling, created safe spaces for him to speak freely, but he shut the doors I longed for him to open.

By June 1984, I was emotionally spent. Mentally drained. Hoping to restore a sense of joy, I planned a simple fishing trip to Norfolk. I brought LeDon and my niece Jocelyn, praying that fresh air and laughter might lift our spirits. Mommy and Aunt Martha came along, excited for the day.

But even that morning, something felt… off.

Mommy mentioned a headache, casually took a Stanback, and brushed it aside like she always did. Still, a heaviness lingered in my spirit.

At Harrison Fishing Pier, in Norfolk, Virginia, she and Aunt Martha stayed behind in the shade while the children and I boarded the boat. I tried to focus on the moment—to laugh, to breathe—but that quiet voice inside wouldn't be silenced.

When we returned hours later, they were still sitting in the same place. My heart dropped. I rushed toward them. Mommy's mouth drooped, her body was sluggish, her gaze distant.

A chill shot through me. Something was terribly wrong.

Without hesitation, I gathered everyone and drove home as fast as I could, panic growing with every mile. As soon as we arrived, I called for an ambulance.

The four of us followed it to the Medical College of Virginia, each second stretching into an eternity. I had barely begun to grieve Daddy's passing—and now this.

When they finally called me into the back, the doctor's expression said it before his words did:

"Your mother has suffered a major stroke."

I broke down. Tears streamed freely, guilt gnawed at me. She'd been with me, hurting—and I hadn't seen it.

She was admitted to the ICU, hooked up to tubes and machines—a painful, surreal sight that drove home how quickly life can shatter. Aunt Martha stood beside me, silent and steady, holding the emotional weight I couldn't bear all

My spirit cracked. My faith wavered.

"What more can I take?" I whispered.
"God, please… give me strength."

Walking in Obedience to the Spirit

As the seasons shifted, so did the rhythm of our lives—we were learning how to navigate loss, embrace healing, and move forward despite the heavy void Daddy left behind.

One afternoon, while visiting Mary Frances, the phone rang. It was Aunt Bert, asking to speak with me. I hesitated as I picked up the receiver, unsure of what she wanted, though her tone carried an urgency I couldn't ignore.

"Hello, Aunt Bert. How are you?" I greeted her warmly.

She responded with quiet desperation. Calling me by my middle name, she said, "Bernadette, I really wish you'd try to get that land sold… I could use my little money.

Her words stirred memories weighted with generations of unresolved history. My great-grandfather, Papa, had passed without leaving a will. With his death, he left behind seven living children and the descendants of those who came before—each one an heir to the estate, which included the family homeplace and several acres of land. For years, that land had been a source of division—tangled in emotions, legal complexities, and lingering resentment.

Frustration welled up inside me. *No way am I about to deal with this family over land,* I thought. I wanted no part in the ongoing drama.

But then—something shifted.

That voice.

The same divine voice that had spoken to me in my darkest moments… when despair once wrapped itself so tightly around my mind that I questioned whether I could go on.

"I am not finished with you yet. I have something else for you to do."

My heart pounded. I swallowed hard.

"God, if this is truly Your calling—if You want me to work with this family—You have to guide me. You have to show me. Because this… this is not something I want to do."

Still, I found myself saying, "I'll think about it."

But my spirit already knew—when God calls, His voice is persistent, and His purpose will not be ignored.

After months of prayer, the answer came with clarity in early spring of 1984: *It was time.*

I reached out to Cousins Jimmy and Annie May and shared the idea of organizing a Christian Family Reunion. Without hesitation, they embraced it wholeheartedly. Their faith and enthusiasm fueled my own and gave me the courage to step into this intimidating task with renewed conviction.

Together, we formed a planning committee—a team of dedicated heirs who understood the importance of legacy:

- **Jimmy Brown** – President
- **Annie Mayo** – Secretary
- **Bill Armstead** – Treasurer
- **Helen Lightfoot** – Program Chairperson
- **Gwen Thornton** – Historian

Other committee members included Mary Lightfoot DePriest, Louise DePriest Barge, Alice Christian Brown, Martha Christian Armstead, George Minor, Christine Lightfoot Marrow, and Mary Frances Hill—each one carrying the legacy of those who came before us.

And then, it happened.
August 31 – September 2, 1984.

It was more than a reunion. It was a healing. A sacred moment where old wounds softened, new bonds formed, and the legacy of our ancestors was celebrated in a way that none of us would forget.

Under the theme **"Tying Our Roots Together,"** we hosted the first Christian Family Reunion—a celebration filled with love, remembrance, and unity.

Family members traveled from across the country, some coming from as far as California, all gathering to honor this sacred occasion.

Four generations stood together—over 250 descendants of Harrison and Octavia Christian—joined not just by blood, but by purpose.

Watching my family laugh, cry, embrace, and reconnect, I knew without a doubt: this was what I was meant to do.

And to think—I almost said no.

But when God speaks, His voice doesn't fade. It finds you, calls you by name, and waits for your answer.

Because of that call—and that obedience—our family was united once more.

The Christian Family Reunion wasn't just an event. It was a turning point. A sacred gathering where we chose healing over hurt, unity over division. It reminded us that even in grief, life carries on—and we must carry each other with it.

Becoming the Healer: From Heartache to Holistic Care

In the wake of Mommy's declining health, my world became a relentless cycle of heartbreak and resilience. Balancing caregiving, motherhood, and work stretched me beyond anything I thought I could endure.

Her passing in September 1986 plunged both me and my son into emotional turmoil—during a season that once brimmed with joy, we found ourselves wrestling with grief that felt unyielding. The loss was raw, deep, and consuming.

And yet, even in those darkest hours, divine mercy manifested through people placed gently in my path. Dr. Christian, Dr. Whitehurst-Cook, and Aunt Martha—each became a steadying presence, their wisdom and compassion helping me begin the long journey of rediscovering my strength.

By New Year's Day of 1987, something within me shifted. Therapy became a lifeline, a sacred space where I began to unravel the knots of sorrow and exhaustion that had bound me. In quiet moments, I could hear the whispers of my ancestors—guiding, nudging, urging me toward a new path.

At the Children's Home Society, the sting of systemic injustice had grown sharper. I began to feel called toward deeper, more transformative work. With faith as my compass, I set my sights on licensure. I wanted more than a career—I wanted a calling rooted in justice, healing, and community.

And so, on **December 19, 1987**, I earned my credential as a **Licensed Clinical Social Worker**—a tangible, hard-won symbol of survival. That piece of paper wasn't just a license. It was proof. That I had endured. That I had transformed pain into purpose.

By the spring of 1988, I stepped fully into that purpose, launching a private counseling practice in Charles City. I focused on serving rural communities—places often overlooked, yet deeply deserving of care.

What had once been my own valley of grief became the very soil in which I planted the seeds of healing for others.

I had become the healer I once needed.

Amid the turbulence of my personal life, change was stirring in my professional world as well. In 1994, I learned that Norfolk State University was preparing to launch the Ethelyn Strong School of Social Work Doctoral Program in the fall of 1995. After prayerful reflection and encouragement from trusted friends and colleagues, I submitted my application. I was deeply honored to be selected as part of the inaugural doctoral cohort at NSU.

But when I shared the news with the contractual clinicians at my private practice, tension quickly surfaced. Beneath the surface of our professional camaraderie, I discovered whispers of a possible hostile takeover. The conflict shook me. Anxiety gripped my heart, and stress clouded my vision. Still, I could not allow fear—or betrayal—to derail what I knew was a calling. I clung to Isaiah 54:17: *"No weapon that is formed against you shall prosper, and every tongue that rises against you in judgment you shall condemn."*

That fall, I officially began my doctoral studies. I had the privilege of learning from some of the most distinguished minds in social work: Drs. Douglas Glasgow, Leon Chestang, Larry Davis, Leon Williams, and Joseph Anderson. But make no mistake—it was grueling. I continued to run my practice during the week while commuting from Quinton to Norfolk every weekend, attending classes from Friday evening to Sunday afternoon. The demands were relentless.

By 1996, I faced a sobering truth: I could not do it all. With a heavy heart, I made the painful decision to close my practice. The thought of stepping away from the community I had so passionately served left me grieving. Unsure of myself and seeking spiritual reassurance, I turned to Dr. Milton Hathaway, pastor of Second Liberty Baptist Church, where I often worshipped. When I confided in him, he responded with calm conviction:

"Sister Thornton, you have no reason to feel bad about your decision. God may have bigger plans for you, and He will open doors for you."

His words were exactly what I needed—divine encouragement to keep going.

Soon after, on April 26, 1996, I received an unexpected blessing: I had been selected by the Council of Higher Education for Virginia to receive the **Commonwealth Graduate Fellowship** for the 1996–1998 academic years. This prestigious award, intended to prepare future faculty for careers in higher education, provided $20,000 in support for full-time study. It was a confirmation that I was right where I needed to be.

That fall, I permanently closed my practice. Though grief lingered, I surrendered to the season I was being called into—one of academic pursuit and professional growth. I completed all my coursework by the end of 1996. Only one challenge remained: the comprehensive exams. Under program policy, students were allowed only two attempts. Failure on both meant dismissal.

I gave it everything I had—but I did not pass either attempt.

The day the termination letter arrived from the program director, the devastation was complete. I was crushed. I had sacrificed so much, and now it felt like I had nothing to show for it. But even in that painful moment, I turned to God, whispering for strength, trusting that my journey was not over.

In the spring of 1997, I attended the Virginia Chapter conference of the National Association of Social Workers in Richmond. There, **Mrs. Cheryl Mathews**, Director of the BSW Program at Christopher Newport University (CNU), was recognized for her contributions to social work education. I almost didn't approach her—my introverted nature tried to hold me back—but something stirred within me. After the program ended, I gathered my courage, walked up to her, and shared my interest in becoming an adjunct instructor.

She smiled and said, "Send me your resume."

I didn't hesitate. I submitted it immediately—and she hired me.

That fall, I stepped into a new calling as an adjunct instructor. What began as a small step forward became the beginning of a transformative new chapter. Teaching would not only renew my purpose—it would restore the part of me I feared had been lost.

Cheryl Mathews, Me, and Dr Joe Healey

Embracing Adversity to Fulfill My Purpose

Still reeling from the disappointment of failing my comprehensive exams, I confided in my physician and dear friend, Dr. Whitehurst-Cook. I explained how overwhelming anxiety had clouded my focus during both attempts, even though I knew the material inside and out. Quietly, I admitted something I had long suspected: that I might have a learning difference that had gone undiagnosed for years.

She listened with warmth and understanding, then gently suggested I meet with Dr. Don Roebuck, a colleague at MCV who specialized in evaluating students with learning challenges. Trusting her guidance, I scheduled an appointment. As I arrived, waves of nervousness washed over me—but his kind demeanor and calm presence instantly put me at ease.

I shared openly about my struggles: the paralyzing anxiety, the inability to focus, and the frustration of knowing I was capable, yet unable to demonstrate it under pressure. After listening attentively, Dr. Roebuck asked if I'd be willing to complete the Amen Adult ADD Symptom Checklist. With nothing to lose, I agreed.

Once I finished, he reviewed my responses with great care. The results revealed elevated scores consistent with symptoms of ADD. As he explained the findings, a wave of relief came over me. My struggle wasn't about intelligence—it had never been. For the first time, there was a name, a reason, an explanation. The burden of self-doubt I had been carrying for years began to lift.

Dr. Roebuck then referred me to Dr. Edward Peck, a respected clinical neuropsychologist, for further evaluation. It was another step forward—another act of courage.

In March 1998, I met with Dr. Peck for a full neuropsychological assessment. The process was long and emotionally taxing. Each task challenged my patience, and the constant self-comparison stirred old insecurities. I pushed through, determined to face the truth.

When it came time to review the results, I sat quietly, bracing myself. Dr. Peck began with words I never expected to hear: I was intelligent. My higher-level reasoning skills were not only intact—they were strong. But he also confirmed that I processed information differently. The assessment revealed irregularities in how I managed auditory input and immediate memory, especially in high-pressure environments.

Words often came too quickly, like water rushing through a narrow channel. I struggled to catch them before they slipped past. I didn't always process sound in real-time the way others could. It wasn't that I wasn't paying attention—I just needed more time to absorb and interpret. In noisy rooms, or during fast-paced conversations, I often lost pieces of meaning. I had learned, long ago, to compensate: I wrote things down. I asked for repetition. I tuned into body language and silences. I listened with my heart as much as my ears.

Some challenges also showed up when my memory had to work hand in hand with my hands and eyes—like organizing visual sequences or following steps. I was slower, but I got there. The issue was never comprehension—it was pace and processing. What the world called a delay, I came to see as my rhythm.

I remember sitting across from Dr. Peck, gripping the edge of my clipboard, muscles tight with anticipation. I had already rehearsed the shame I thought was coming. Instead, his words came gently—like light filtering through trees.

"Your thinking abilities range from average to superior in several areas," he said.

I blinked. *Superior?* In some areas?

I had always seen my struggles as proof that something was wrong with me. But in that moment, I heard something different: that my brain wasn't broken—it was simply wired to operate on its own terms. That realization shifted everything.

I stopped trying to fit into someone else's mold and started embracing the way I was designed. I began writing more. Remembering more. Trusting more. I gave myself permission to move at my own pace, and in doing so, I found my voice—not just as a learner, but as a healer and a storyteller.

What I once saw as limitations, I now recognized as tools—unique instruments crafted for a specific purpose. And in learning how to honor them, I began to honor myself.

Challenging Barriers to Academic Equity

Throughout my doctoral journey, I immersed myself in Social Welfare Policy. Under the guidance of the esteemed Dr. Glasgow, I both studied and taught the subject—serving as an undergraduate policy instructor at CNU. I was thoroughly familiar with the Americans with Disabilities Act (ADA) of 1990 and fully understood the legal obligations of institutions to accommodate students with learning differences. Yet, as I progressed through my research, a sobering truth emerged: Norfolk State University and its School of Social Work had no structured program to support students with learning disabilities. Worse still, the institution was not in compliance with federal law.

The realization struck a deep chord. I couldn't ignore it—not just as a student, but as an advocate for equity. Determined to address the issue, I compiled my research, my personal experiences, and evidence of institutional shortcomings. Then I did what I hoped others would be encouraged to do: I knocked on the highest door.

President Dr. Marie McDemmond had an open-door policy, and I intended to use it. When I finally sat across from her, my heart beat with urgency and resolve. I laid everything bare—how the doctoral program failed students with learning disabilities, how the university had no infrastructure in place for academic accommodations, and how these failures violated the ADA.

She listened quietly, her expression unreadable. When I finished, she simply responded, "Thank you for sharing your concerns. I will get back with you."

That was it. No promises, no clear next steps. Just a vague acknowledgment.

Days passed. Then came a letter from the School of Social Work: I had been granted an opportunity to appeal my case before the doctoral committee. I could make a formal argument for the right to retake my comprehensive exam. It was a small opening—but it was something.

What weighed heavily, however, was that Dr. McDemmond never followed up. I never heard from her again.

The appeal meeting loomed ahead, and with it came a swell of anxiety. My advisor and dissertation committee chair, Dr. Glasgow, was unable to attend. The absence of his presence felt like armor missing from a warrior—like I was walking into battle alone.

As I stepped into the sterile conference room, I was met with blank expressions and bureaucratic coldness. No encouragement. No warmth. Just procedure.

Still, I steadied myself and spoke. I didn't just advocate for myself—I spoke on behalf of every student whose needs had been ignored, every learner who had faced institutional indifference. I laid out my case with clarity, citing legal precedent, academic evidence, and personal testimony. Every question felt like an interrogation. Every moment, a test of resolve.

And in the end—I won.

The committee granted me the chance to retake the exam. Even more significantly, two other students—who had previously been denied—were also granted permission to retake theirs.

At that moment, I knew that my battle had not been in vain. My voice had not only carved out a second chance for myself but had created a path for others. I had challenged a broken system—and the system had budged.

That fall, after passing my comprehensive exam, I began drafting my dissertation proposal. I also returned my focus to personal well-being and transitioned into a full-time instructor role in the Social Work Department at CNU.

Needing renewal, I planned something special for someone who had given so much of herself. I took my 87-year-old grandmother—who had spent her life working as a live-in housekeeper—on her first vacation. We traveled to Martha's Vineyard to visit my cousin Larry and his wife. For her, it was a once-in-a-lifetime experience. She laughed, explored, and reflected. She often spoke of that trip in the years that followed.

It reminded me that healing doesn't always come through triumph alone—sometimes, it comes through honoring those who paved the way for us.

Overcoming Adversity on the Path to Purpose

The two years following my proposal defense were marked by unrelenting challenges that tested the limits of my perseverance. Coordinating with my dissertation committee became a drawn-out struggle, riddled with delays and uncertainty. Thankfully, Dr. Glasgow—my dedicated committee chair—ultimately rallied the members and secured a defense date, enabling me to successfully defend my proposal in April 2000.

But while my academic journey pressed forward, my personal life demanded just as much strength.

On May 15, 2000, tragedy came crashing in with merciless finality. The phone rang, and before I even answered, I felt it—something was wrong. Cousin Bill's voice, strained and trembling, confirmed what my heart already knew: his son, Junnie—William Jr.—was gone.

A motorcycle accident had taken his life at just 32 years old.

It was inconceivable. Junnie had fought tooth and nail to overcome addiction, and he'd emerged with purpose—as a recovery sponsor and mentor for others trying to reclaim their lives. He had become a light for those navigating darkness, a living example of redemption and resilience. And now, that light had been extinguished.

Without hesitation, I packed my bags. I knew Bill and his family would need every ounce of strength and love I could bring. But how does one comfort a grieving father? How do you hold together someone whose world has been shattered?

The weight of sorrow met me at the door. It was thick in the air, pressing into every room. Bill's face said everything his voice couldn't—anguish etched into every line.

Grief was a constant presence, uninvited and immovable. The community grieved with us, mourning a man who had touched so many lives and lifted so many hearts. His absence was not quiet—it echoed.

We clung to his memory—his laughter, his wisdom, his remarkable transformation. We spoke his name aloud, refusing to let his spirit fade.

He was not remembered as a man who lost a battle, but as a warrior who fought with unwavering courage.

And though his life ended far too soon, Junnie's story didn't stop there. His impact endured—in the lives he touched and the hope he passed on. His legacy, like his light, remained.

At the same time, I was navigating another emotional burden: managing my grandmother's finances and healthcare. Though I stepped in with love and a sense of duty, my decision was met with resistance from my birth mother and siblings, adding a painful layer of conflict. Still, ensuring my grandmother's well-being was non-negotiable. Hiring my cousin Mousie as her live-in caregiver proved to be one of the few comforting decisions during that turbulent season.

Just as I began regaining momentum with my dissertation, another blow arrived. In June, Dr. Glasgow informed me that he would not be returning to NSU—and I would need to find a new committee chair. After years of building my research under his guidance, the news was devastating. Starting over with someone unfamiliar was overwhelming. To complicate matters further, financial aid issues and administrative roadblocks at the School of Social Work only deepened my stress.

Still, I pushed forward.

In 2001, determined to bring joy amid the storms, I planned a celebration for my grandmother's 90th birthday—an event to honor her lifetime of love and service. Surrounded by family and friends, the day overflowed with laughter and gratitude. One of the most moving moments was the surprise appearance of the Ray family, for whom she had worked for over 50 years. Their presence was a powerful tribute to the deep bonds she had cultivated.

Yet even this joyful day carried shadows. Her daughter, Mary Frances, along with my sisters Pinkie and Mookie, chose not to attend. Their absence was a sharp and painful reminder of the unresolved fractures in our family.

That same year, my son—then 27—surprised me with an unexpected announcement. Fresh off the triumph of completing my dissertation proposal, I was stunned when he calmly told me he wanted to return to school—this time, to study mortuary science at John Tyler Community College.

Until then, he'd been building a stable career as a pharmacy technician after his military service. This pivot was completely unforeseen.

He hinted that he needed help with tuition. With a teasing smile and just a touch of skepticism, I asked, "What, you want me to foot the bill for you?" Though I joked, I wasn't entirely convinced he could manage the process alone. So I stepped in. I drove to JTCC, paid the tuition in full, and handed him the documents he needed for financial aid.

It was a leap of faith—on both our parts. But he rose to the occasion. He threw himself into his studies and, to our surprise and pride, excelled. After completing his coursework, he immediately secured an apprenticeship. Watching him grow into this new chapter reminded me that sometimes the most unexpected paths lead to the most meaningful outcomes.

As the 2002–2003 academic year approached, the pressure was at its peak. Every ounce of my energy was devoted to completing my dissertation in time for my defense in April 2003. Dr. Leon Williams became an indispensable guide, offering consistent support and wisdom as I refined my research.

After my defense, I learned something that moved me deeply: Dr. Glasgow—though no longer at NSU—had personally asked Dr. Williams to ensure I had the support I needed to finish. That act of unseen kindness reminded me that even in adversity, people were standing in my corner.

On April 14, 2003, at the age of 52, I defended my dissertation: *"An Exploratory Study of the Influence of Family Environmental Characteristics and Peer Influence on Delinquency Among Black Females."* The journey had taken eight years—eight years of grief, struggle, sacrifice, and relentless hope.

And I did it.

On June 10, 2003, I was awarded my DSW/PhD in Social Work.

That day was more than a milestone. It was a declaration: that faith, persistence, and purpose can prevail over even the harshest trials. That no matter how winding the road, the destination is worth the journey.

Dr. Glasgow - my professor &mentor

CHAPTER 11

A DREAM REALIZED: MY JOURNEY TO THE HEART OF AFRICA

My Soul's Journey to Kenya

During my tenure at Christopher Newport University, I was fortunate to be surrounded by colleagues who valued both professional and personal growth. They championed curiosity, exploration, and the courage to step beyond the familiar. One of those colleagues, Professor Lea Pellett from the Sociology Department, regularly led study abroad trips, offering students and faculty alike the opportunity to broaden their horizons.

I had always dreamed of setting foot on the Motherland —Africa. That longing was more than a travel wish; it lived deep within me, woven into the fabric of my identity. The stories, the culture, the history—I felt connected to it all before I ever touched the soil.

One day, Professor Pellett shared news that made my heart race: she was organizing a trip to Kenya in December 2004. In that moment, the dream I had carried for so long suddenly felt within reach.

The thought of traveling to Kenya—breathing in its air, standing on ancestral land, hearing the rhythms of life in a place I had always imagined—filled me with anticipation. But this wasn't just about visiting. It was about connection. Understanding. Embracing a part of myself that had long been calling out to be remembered.

As the trip moved from possibility to reality, a storm of emotions swirled inside me—excitement, nervousness, and deep, abiding gratitude. I knew this journey would be transformative. It wasn't merely a trip; it was a spiritual homecoming.

The drive from Newport News to Dulles Airport in Washington, D.C., felt momentous—like I was crossing a threshold into something sacred. As we boarded British Airways, my heart pounded with anticipation. A brief layover in Amsterdam gave me time to reflect, to steady myself for what was to come. And after more than sixteen hours in the sky, I felt it—homecoming.

As we descended toward Nairobi, I gazed out the window in silence, overcome with emotion. There it was—Kenya. The Motherland. The land my ancestors once walked. The place my soul had longed for. Stepping off the plane, the air greeted me—crisp and pure, unlike anything I had ever breathed before. My chest tightened. I was here.

Passing through customs, I felt the energy of the land embrace me. And then—music. Rhythm. Movement. African dancers welcomed us with drums and songs. "Welcome home, my sister," they sang, their voices rich with history and belonging. At that moment, I was no longer just a visitor. I was returning. And I had never felt so free. So whole.

Stanley, our driver, and Agnes, our guide and coordinator, greeted us warmly, efficiently loading our luggage while I stood in silent awe. The sights, the sounds, the embrace of the culture—every detail wrapped around me. Kenya was already beginning to change me.

But then came a quick lesson in reality. Ever budget-conscious, Professor Pellett had arranged for modest accommodations. As we arrived at the hotel, my heart sank—no elevator, and three flights of stairs stood between me and my room. My arthritic hip throbbed from exhaustion.

It was summer in Kenya—hot and unrelenting. There was no air conditioning. The toilets barely worked; we had to fetch water from the sink and pour it in to flush. Mosquito nets hung from the ceiling—our only protection against malaria and yellow fever.

Still, as I lay beneath that net that night, sticky and sore, I felt something profound: gratitude. I was here. I was home. And my soul had never felt more alive.

After a single night in Nairobi, we rose before dawn to begin our long drive to the Maasai Mara. The cool morning air hummed softly as the city stirred awake. We moved quickly, hoping to beat the day's heat. The van buzzed with quiet excitement—but within me was something more. While my colleagues viewed this as an exciting adventure, I knew I was experiencing something deeper: a return. For them, this was exploration. For me, it was remembrance.

As our van rumbled over unpaved roads, the terrain unfolded before us—raw, untouched, ancient. Each bump reminded me we were entering a world untouched by the speed and noise of the West.

And then the wild appeared, as if summoned: lions basking in golden light, zebras grazing on rich green fields, gazelles moving with effortless grace. These animals, unbothered by our presence, were exactly where they belonged. There was peace in their freedom. Power in their stillness. It was sacred.

Villages dotted the road. Life happened around us—vendors arranging produce and hand-crafted goods with quiet mastery. Children in brightly colored uniforms walked in small groups, their voices full of laughter and song. Daily life unfolded in the open, with rhythm and ease, deeply connected to the land.

The simplicity, the authenticity, the deep-rooted harmony between people and place—it grounded me. I wasn't merely observing Kenya. I was becoming part of it.

Later, I found myself beneath the shade of wide, ancient trees, their branches wrapped around me like the arms of grandmothers long past. I let my hands rest in the soil, sacred and storied. The wind whispered—not in English, not in Swahili, but in knowing. It spoke of survival, triumph, resilience. This was not just dirt—it was history. And I was touching it.

Children's laughter rang out—untamed and unfiltered—filling the afternoon with joy. Elders sat in quiet circles, not demanding attention, but holding it with the weight of their presence. Their eyes met mine—not with curiosity, but recognition. They did not know my name, but they knew my spirit.

And in that moment, I knew too.

Though I had lived across oceans and generations, the essence of me had never left this land. The truth struck me: I wasn't discovering something new—I was remembering something ancient. Something that had always been mine.

When the time came to leave, I did not feel an ending. I felt a beginning.

Africa had spoken. The Motherland had called me back to myself. I returned with a certainty I had never known—that my life, my path, had always been divinely written.

Under the vast Kenyan sky, I made a promise: this was not goodbye.

I would return. And when I did, I would bring my Black brothers and sisters with me—those who yearned for home, for wholeness, for the knowing that cannot be taught, only remembered.

Because home is not always where you are born.

Sometimes, home is where your spirit has always belonged.

Walking in My Truth

Upon my return to the United States, the crisp air of early spring carried both familiarity and quiet transformation. It was the start of the Spring 2005 semester, and as I stepped onto campus, the weight of expectation pressed against me—one I had long grown used to at Christopher Newport University. But this time, something within me had shifted.

Walking into the classroom that first day back, everything looked the same—the walls, the desks, the mix of eager and hesitant student faces. Yet the woman standing before them was not the same.

Working at a predominantly white institution (PWI), I had spent years navigating spaces that demanded constant validation. I had learned to prove my worth in environments that subtly, and at times overtly, resisted full acceptance. Higher education was supposed to be a beacon of knowledge, openness, and inclusion. Yet too often, I found myself pushing against invisible walls—barriers that tried to limit, confine, and define me.

But Kenya had given me something far more enduring than academic credentials or institutional approval. It had gifted me an unshakable truth about who I was.

The land had spoken to me—not in a language of words, but of deep ancestral knowing. It reminded me that my existence was purposeful, that I was not made to shrink, to contort myself to fit a mold that had never been designed for me. I did not need to prove my intelligence. It was already mine. I did not need to ask for permission to take up space. My ancestors had already granted me that right.

So as I stood before my students, a new certainty settled into my bones. My voice no longer searched for approval; it stood firm in its knowing. I was not just an educator—I was a vessel of truth, a carrier of generational wisdom, a witness to legacy.

Kenya had not changed who I was. It had revealed what had always been true. I was not merely somebody. I was divinely created, walking in purpose

A Heart Shattered: The Unbearable Weight of Loss

Tragedy struck our family once again—swift, merciless, and cruel. It came like a brutal storm, ripping through our lives without warning. And when it passed, it left behind a silence so heavy that even time felt unbearable.

It was an ordinary day when Cousin Mousie—the steadfast caretaker who had so lovingly devoted herself to my grandmother—received a phone call that would fracture her world. The words on the other end landed with a cold, cruel finality: her daughter, Waynette, only 32 years old, had been found deceased.

I watched the color drain from Mousie's face as if the very essence of her spirit had been ripped away. Her body folded inward, clutching her chest as if she could somehow hold together the pieces of a heart that had just shattered. A mother should never have to bury her child—it defies the natural order. It's a cruel reversal, a tear in the fabric of life no parent is prepared to mend.

She didn't speak. The silence between us thickened, dense with sorrow, too weighted for words. The air itself grew suffocating, as if grief had taken form and settled into the room with us.

I reached for her—but how does one comfort the inconsolable? What can you offer when the pain goes beyond human touch or comprehension? There was no answer, no remedy, no words strong enough to soften the blow of such profound loss. I could only be there—present, grounded in the weight of the moment—bearing witness to her heartbreak.

At first, she didn't cry. Her body remained frozen, trembling with shock as her mind struggled to grasp the truth. And then, slowly, like a dam breaking under unbearable pressure, the sobs came.

They were not gentle.

They were guttural, primal—tearing through her with a force that shook the room. The sound was not just sorrow—it was devastation incarnate. It was the sound of a soul grieving its other half.

Her pain became mine. It became ours. The loss of Waynette was not just a blow to Mousie; it tore through the fabric of our family. Waynette had been loved, cherished. And now, she was gone.

There was nothing we could do—nothing but bear the unbearable together. We sat with the sorrow, held space for the grief, and let it move as it needed to. Because when someone you love is taken too soon, no logic, no prayer, no ritual can erase the ache. You simply stand in the storm with those who remain.

In the end, love and loss are woven from the same cloth. And when love is deep, loss echoes louder. Sometimes, all we can offer is presence— sacred, silent, and full of compassion.

CHAPTER 12

PURPOSE, SERVICE, AND STRENGTH

The Testament of Perseverance and Faith

The two years that followed unfolded with a rhythm both liberating and demanding. After the relentless pursuit of my doctorate, the academic weight finally lifted, allowing me to breathe differently—to live without the constant pressure of defending, refining, and proving my scholarship. But in academia, peace is always fleeting. There is always another battle waiting.

The looming mantra of "publish or perish" hovered like a storm cloud—persistent, impersonal, and impossible to ignore. Tenure was the goal, but the rules were unyielding: without publications in peer-reviewed journals, my position at Christopher Newport University remained uncertain. I hadn't dedicated my life to education for accolades or prestige. I taught to serve, to uplift, to transform. But the academy valued citations over service, research over relationships, theory over lived reality.

Still, if I was going to remain in this space—and use it as a platform for the very change I believed in—I would have to play the game. So, I did. I presented at conferences and led workshops, inserting my voice into rooms where it had long been absent or ignored. I stepped into academic arenas not to chase prestige but to claim space that should have always included voices like mine.

Then, on April 22, 2005, my world shifted in a way no journal publication ever could. My grandson, Jaden, was born. And from the moment I laid eyes on him, I knew—deep in the marrow of my being—that he was a divine gift. He wasn't just another branch on our family tree; he was a soul sent from heaven, wrapped in light and purpose.

When I held him for the first time, warmth radiated through me, seeping into the deepest corners of my spirit. His tiny fingers curled tightly around mine, as if he already understood our bond. His breath was soft, his presence powerful. That quiet, miraculous moment affirmed what I already believed: love transcends time, generations, and even understanding. Jaden wasn't just my grandson. He was a promise—a manifestation of God's enduring grace.

That summer, I found renewed purpose through service. I volunteered with the Remote Area Medical (RAM) Clinic in Southwest Virginia, alongside Dr. Whitehurst-Cook and her medical students. RAM, dedicated to delivering healthcare to the underserved, stripped away academic theory and forced me to face the rawness of rural poverty. As we arrived at the old fairgrounds in Wise County, I was stunned. A line of hundreds stretched nearly two miles—men, women, children— waiting under the sweltering sun for basic medical, dental, and vision care.

No statistic could prepare me for the reality of those faces.

Nearly 20 percent of the county lived below the poverty line, but the data did no justice to the dignity I saw in those who had waited for hours, hoping to be seen. Registering patients may have seemed like a simple task, but to me, it felt sacred. This was where service lived—on the ground, in the dust, in the shared humanity of need and care. It reminded me why I entered this field to begin with.

Later that spring, my university awarded me a professional development grant. With it, I returned to Wise County—this time with my students: Katy Deitz-Carbaugh, Amelia Long-Williams, and Tremetris Davis-Harrell. Together, we conducted research on the intersections of substance abuse, unemployment, and mental health disparities in Appalachian communities. Our work culminated in a published paper, but for once, the publication wasn't about prestige. It was purpose—scholarship in service to the people.

As the fall semester approached, I began planning a second journey to Kenya. The pull of the Motherland hadn't faded—it had intensified. But my hip pain had worsened to the point where walking, let alone flying across continents, became unthinkable. For the first time, I had to pause. I had to choose health over passion.

With resolve, I requested sick leave and prepared for what was inevitable: hip replacement surgery. Dr. Anthony Carter, a highly respected orthopedic surgeon in Hampton, was recommended to me. After one meeting, I knew he was the right choice—the one entrusted to help me walk freely again.

In October 2005, I underwent surgery. It was uneventful, smooth—just as I had prayed. My cousin Shortie, though retired from nursing, came down to Newport News and cared for me with tenderness and discipline. For two weeks, she nurtured me back to strength, ensuring I didn't just heal but thrived. Her faith in my recovery never wavered. With her gentle encouragement, I was soon up and moving again, eyes already set on my next horizon.

Though my body was still healing, my spirit was already in Kenya. I could feel it—the tug, the calling. And I knew this next journey to the Motherland would be deeper, more transformative than the first.

What I didn't realize was that this season of stillness and recovery wasn't a detour. It was preparation. Kenya awaited, but so did something more:

a new version of myself, shaped not just by pain and perseverance, but by the unwavering grace that had followed me all along.

A Journey of Service and Purpose

When I boarded the plane in December 2005, a familiar excitement stirred in my chest—but this time, it carried a deeper resonance. I was not traveling alone. With me were Shortie—my rock during recovery—and Dr. James McCain, the dentist I had worked for before returning to academia. Their presence added weight and purpose to this journey. We brought not only our renewed spirits, but medical supplies—tools of healing, hope, and dignity.

Word spread quickly upon our arrival in the village. Within hours, people began to gather—some walking miles under the sun, driven only by the hope of being seen by a doctor or nurse. Their resilience left me speechless. Their trust was humbling. These were individuals whose medical needs had long gone unmet, pushed aside by the cruel arithmetic of access and affordability. Yet they came, not with demands, but with open hearts, believing in the hands that came to serve them.

The weight of the moment did not escape me. This was more than healthcare—it was an offering of solidarity. Each screening, each consultation was a quiet affirmation: *I see you. I honor you. You matter.* Their dignity was not something to be restored—it had never left. Our work simply acknowledged it.

In their eyes, I saw the reflection of my ancestors. In their stories, I heard echoes of my own. And as I tended to their needs, my spirit stretched wider. My purpose sharpened. The barriers between giver and receiver blurred, replaced by something more sacred: connection.

The trip was an overwhelming success—a living testament to the power of service rooted in love. And as we departed, my heart echoed the same vow I had made a year before: *I will return.*

Because this was never just a trip. It was a calling.

And so, we did return the following year—stronger in our mission, deeper in our conviction that service is not an event, but a way of being.

Pictures of my CNU students /mentees working at the RAM clinic collecting research data

Tremetrius Davis-Harrell - Collecting Data

Katy Deitz-Carbaugh- Collecting Data

Amelia Long-Williams- Collecting Data

Me and CNU students with U.S. Senator Mark Warner
(Former Governor of Virginia)

CHAPTER 13

WALKING THROUGH PAIN WITH PURPOSE

Faith Through the Flames: Rising from Grief

The beginning of 2006 marked what I hoped would be a season of stability and clarity. Stepping out on faith, I purchased a condominium in Newport News, Virginia—a space I believed would be home for years to come. Yet even as I decorated the walls and settled into the rhythm of new routines, a quiet stirring in my spirit whispered: *Your journey is far from over.*

Each week, I made the drive from Newport News to Richmond to visit my grandmother and Cousin Mousie—the devoted caregiver who had, with tireless love, ensured my grandmother's comfort and well-being. Those visits became sacred—moments of reconnection, a chance to express gratitude, and a quiet reminder to Mousie that her sacrifices had not gone unnoticed.

But as winter gave way to spring, subtle changes in Mousie began to concern me. She had always been petite, seemingly untouched by the effects of age or appetite. Now, though, she spoke of unfamiliar aches and pains. Her belly swelled unnaturally, as if cradling a life that did not exist. I watched with growing unease, torn between concern and the desire to honor her deep-rooted sense of privacy.

And then came the call—the one that shattered the illusion of normalcy.

Mousie had been rushed to the hospital.

My heart pounded as I sped down the highway, prayers tumbling from my lips like a lifeline. When I entered her hospital room, the air felt heavy with unspeakable truth. She sat on the edge of the bed, frail but calm. Her eyes met mine, and I saw it—she knew.

But instead of fear, there was faith. She lifted her hands and said, with quiet strength, "I know Jesus."

Even in suffering, she praised Him—for His grace, His mercy, His presence. I stood in awe, overcome by the purity of her belief. Tears blurred my vision as I reached for her hand.

"I love you," I whispered.

She smiled softly. "I love you too."

That was the last time we would speak.

On March 20, 2006, just shy of her 55th birthday, Mousie passed away. Her absence carved a canyon of grief in my heart that words still fail to describe.

But grief, however deep, did not permit me to pause. I had to act—to secure care for my grandmother in Mousie's absence, to protect her peace in a world that felt suddenly unstable. With no support from my birth mother or siblings, the responsibility rested squarely on me.

Vann, Mousie's brother, and I moved quickly, forming a plan to relocate our grandmother and his mother, Aunt Lois, into Tony's vacant home. In exchange for rent and caregiving, they would have a safe, loving place to live.

But the plan unraveled.

Outside influence persuaded Tony to revoke the arrangement, and the betrayal of that broken promise devastated my grandmother and Aunt Lois. They were once again displaced—unsettled and heartbroken.

There was no time to mourn the loss of that plan. Vann and his wife, Eunice, took in Aunt Lois. I leaned on my background in gerontology, making call after call in search of a facility that offered not just care, but dignity. I needed a place where my grandmother could *thrive*.

God answered.

St. Francis Nursing Care Facility in Newport News, walking distance from my home, became her sanctuary. And as if divinely orchestrated, the Director of Social Work was my former field instructor. Her assigned social worker? Elizabeth Koenig-Combs—a former student of mine. I exhaled. My grandmother was in the hands of those I trusted.

For five years, she lived at St. Francis, receiving not only professional care but constant love. And I was there—every single day. Our bond, tested by time and loss, remained steadfast. Those simple moments—holding her hand, brushing her hair, whispering prayers—became the threads that held me together.

Looking back, I see how fire refines. The grief, the responsibility, the unexpected turns—all of it became sacred instruction. I learned that family is not always defined by blood, but by presence. By sacrifice. By the people who show up in both your sorrow and your strength.

Finding Strength in Life's Trials

As summer's warmth gave way to the crisp air of autumn, the 2006 academic semester loomed on the horizon. It should have been a time of new beginnings, yet instead, it brought the looming weight of my tenure review. My spirit, already worn thin by grief and physical pain, braced for another trial.

With lingering issues in my left hip and a quiet fear that leaving Christopher Newport University might cost me my healthcare benefits, I made a strategic decision: I would undergo a second hip replacement and request sick leave for the fall semester. I needed time to recover—physically, emotionally, and spiritually.

Then, in the stillness of my healing, a letter arrived from the Provost's Office. Its tone was cold, its message clear: I was not being recommended for tenure. A meeting was scheduled during Christmas break with the Provost and the Dean of the College of Humanities and Social Sciences. The outcome wasn't a surprise—I had sensed it coming—but seeing it in writing struck a painful, definitive chord.

In the days leading up to that meeting, I turned to prayer with fierce devotion. Romans 8:28 and Philippians 4:13 became my anchors:

"All things work together for the good of those who love God."
"I can do all things through Christ who strengthens me."

With my walker steadying my steps and Scripture strengthening my soul, I entered that meeting with the quiet resolve of Shadrach, Meshach, and Abednego—unbent, unburned, and unshaken in my faith.

The Provost delivered the decision plainly: my tenure was denied. I would be permitted to return for the 2007–2008 academic year, but my time at CNU would not continue beyond that. After the two-minute explanation, he asked, with barely concealed formality, "Anything you would like to say?"

I glanced at the Dean, searching for a word of support, a flicker of acknowledgement—but he offered only a curt, "No."

Then I turned back to the Provost. And in that moment, from the deepest well of grace and dignity, I found my voice.

"I am disappointed and deeply hurt," I said, my tone calm but resolute. "I poured 125% of my heart and soul into this university. But I also want to express my gratitude for the professional and personal growth I experienced here. I believe that when one door closes, God opens another."

Silence filled the room. A heavy silence—not of dismissal, but of respect. I stood, excused myself, and walked out—carrying both the sting of rejection and the spark of faith.

Outside, as cold winter air kissed my face, I whispered a prayer into the wind:

"God, You know I need a job. And I know You haven't brought me this far to leave me now."

Even through pain and uncertainty, my heart clung to that promise.

As I approached my car, still reeling from the meeting, I felt a sudden nudge in my spirit—a whisper, soft but unmistakable:

"Go to your office and call Virginia State University."

I paused. Was I imagining things?

Virginia State didn't even have a social work program anymore—its accreditation had been lost years prior. What could possibly be waiting for me there?

Still, the whisper persisted.

I turned around, returned to my office, and picked up the phone.

To my surprise, Dr. Cheryl Stampley, Director of the BSW Social Work Program, answered directly. I introduced myself, offered a brief summary of my credentials, and before I could even finish, she said,

"We've been looking for someone with your background for six months."

It felt like the heavens had cracked open. A door I hadn't even known existed now stood wide before me. She urged me to submit my CV and application immediately.

I sat in stunned silence, the weight of that moment settling in. Just hours ago, I had walked out of a meeting that closed one chapter. Now, with breathtaking clarity, a new one had already begun.

John 14:13–14 echoed in my soul:

"Ask in the Lord's name, and it will be given."

And indeed, it had.

In that moment, I understood more deeply than ever before: when one door closes, God opens another.

And sometimes, all He needs is a heart willing to walk through it.

CHAPTER 14

STEPPING INTO DIVINE PURPOSE

A Journey of Faith, Transition, and Miraculous Grace

As 2007 dawned, I felt an unshakable certainty deep within my spirit: this would be my year of completion. The number seven carries divine significance—symbolizing wholeness, fulfillment, and spiritual perfection. After years of trials, loss, and pressing forward through adversity, I sensed that I had passed the tests life had laid before me. It was time to step into the next chapter with full trust in the One who had carried me this far.

Looking back on my journal entries from that pivotal year, I now see the fingerprints of God on every page. His grace and mercy covered me like a shield. Through every hardship, He sent His majestic angels to guide my steps—never once forsaking me in my moments of doubt or weariness.

Journal Entry: May 15, 2007

Oh, Heavenly Father, I come this morning with thanksgiving in my heart and spirit. I give You all the praise and glory. As I reflect on last week, You truly blessed me and my family—God, You are awesome! Oh, how I love

You. You promised that Your Word would not return void. My son, LeDon, graduated this past weekend, and it was such a glorious occasion. We lifted our voices in praise, giving You all the honor. Lord, I ask that You continue to walk with me on this journey called life. Guide me, Father. I just want to do Your will. Again, I find myself at a crossroads, seeking Your divine direction. Order my steps, Lord.

Journal Entry: May 16, 2007

Father, Father, I come again this morning, thanking You for Your goodness and mercy. I ask for the forgiveness of my sins. I am so grateful for all that You have done in my life and the lives of my family members. Thank You for delivering my son and bringing his dreams to fruition. He finished his college courses and, Almighty God, I lift my hands in praise. As I stand on the brink of a new path, I seek Your guidance. Lord, I know You are the God who pours out the blessings of heaven upon those who ask in Your name. I surrender myself to You—use me for Your purpose, Lord.

Today, I completed my application for a faculty position at Virginia State University. If it is Your will, I ask that You anoint the process with Your Holy Spirit. Prepare me for all You have called me to do, so I may fulfill Your divine plan.

As the weeks passed, a peace I could not explain began to settle deep within me. It was the kind of peace Paul spoke of—*"the peace of God, which surpasses all understanding."* My heart no longer raced with fear. I had come to a sacred stillness—a knowing that my life was divinely orchestrated.

And then, on **October 5, 2007**, another miracle unfolded.

Against all odds, my son LeDon met every requirement, surpassed every challenge, and passed the Funeral Director's Licensure Exam. It was a moment of triumph—not just for him, but for our entire family. Mark

10:27 rang true once again: *"With men it is impossible, but not with God; for with God, all things are possible."*

Then, in late November, the call came.

Dr. Cheryl Stampley reached out and formally offered me a faculty position at Virginia State University. The role I had prayed for, hoped for, and prepared my heart to receive was now mine.

"Could you begin in the January 2008 semester?" she asked.

My spirit rejoiced, but my conscience paused. Though I was ready to step into this divine assignment, I also felt compelled to honor my commitment to CNU. I had students who depended on me, and colleagues who had journeyed beside me. Integrity required me to finish what I had started.

I explained this to Dr. Stampley, and she responded with grace and understanding.

"Well then," she said warmly, "would you consider joining us after the Spring 2008 semester?"

In that moment, I knew—God had already paved the way. There was no need to rush, no need to push. The door was open, and my name was already written on it.

Lessons in Growth, Transition, and Unwavering Determination

As 2008 unfolded, I could feel a shift in the air—an undeniable sense that something pivotal was on the horizon. It was a season brimming with possibility, a time for healing, clarity, and long-awaited inner peace. After years marked by hardship, loss, and profound transformation,

I was finally stepping into a space where new doors were opening—personally, professionally, and spiritually.

The spring semester passed in a blur of classes, students, and daily obligations, but underneath the routine, I carried a quiet knowing: my time at Christopher Newport University was drawing to a close. I wrestled with how and when to share the news with Cheryl—that I had accepted a contract with Virginia State University and would be leaving at the end of the term. The thought sat heavily on my heart. Cheryl had been more than a colleague. She was a mentor, a guide, and a steady hand in seasons of uncertainty.

Under her leadership, I had gained a deep understanding of the inner workings of higher education—from the complexities of accreditation and program development to the subtle but powerful influence of professional networks. She had opened doors that allowed me to stretch my knowledge and broaden my perspective, including opportunities to attend the Baccalaureate Program Directors (BPD) Conference and the Council on Social Work Education (CSWE) Annual Meetings. In those spaces, I engaged with educators and administrators from across the country—voices shaping the future of social work.

In March 2008, I finally found the courage to share my news. To my surprise, she received it with nothing but warmth and encouragement. There was no hint of disappointment, only genuine excitement for the new chapter ahead. Her response reaffirmed what I had long felt in my spirit: this transition was not only right—it was divinely timed.

In one final act of generosity, she offered her support, asking what she could do to help ease my departure and ensure a smooth transition. Her grace reminded me that mentorship is a sacred gift—and that true leaders make room for others to rise.

As the semester came to a close, I paused to reflect—not just on the changes ahead, but on the journey that had led me here. My faith had been my compass through every storm, guiding me through loss and uncertainty with the quiet assurance that *all things work together for good*—if I remained faithful, grateful, and committed to "following the process."

My years at CNU had not been easy, but they had been meaningful. I formed friendships that would remain etched in my heart, and I stood in classrooms where my purpose took shape and form. I worked to create a space of empowerment and possibility—for students to know they were seen, heard, and valued. I reminded them, over and over, that their obstacles did not define them. Their potential did.

Through the work, the challenges, and the quiet triumphs, I came to know resilience—not just in my own life, but in the lives of those I had the honor to teach and uplift. And as I turned the page on this chapter, I carried one profound truth with me:

Every ending is simply the beginning of something greater.

Coming Full Circle: A Return to Purpose

On July 15, 2008—exactly thirty-eight years after being placed on academic probation at Virginia State University—I returned to campus, not as a struggling student, but as a faculty member holding a doctoral degree. The contrast was striking; the moment, monumental. This wasn't just another step in my career—it was a divine appointment, an answered prayer shaped by decades of perseverance, spiritual guidance, and the sacrifices of those who paved the way before me.

As I arrived, gratitude saturated every corner of my being. Every challenge, every hard-won lesson, every quiet triumph had led me to this moment. When I walked away from VSU in 1970, I never could have imagined the winding path that would one day bring me back— but God knew. And it was my faith that carried me here.

At first, I was unaware of the tensions simmering beneath the surface. Faculty and administration were embroiled in deep conflict. Not long after my arrival, Dr. Cheryl Stampley's husband—the university's provost—was asked to resign. The ripple effects were swift and undeniable. Dr. Stampley herself stepped down in early 2009, leaving a significant void in leadership. At the time, Dr. Andrew Kanu served as Dean of the College of Humanities and Social Sciences, and Dr. Julius Malcan chaired the Department of Sociology, Social Work, and Criminal Justice.

In the wake of Dr. Stampley's departure, I was presented with an opportunity that would shape the next phase of my professional journey: the position of Director of the Social Work Program. I accepted without hesitation, stepping into the role with clarity of purpose and a substantial raise. It felt like more than a promotion—it was a call to serve.

As Director, I devoted myself to advancing the Council on Social Work Education (CSWE) national accreditation process—an essential step in securing the program's future. But not everyone grasped the complexity or importance of this work. The accreditation process was rigorous, meticulous, and required full departmental cooperation. Without it, I often found myself pushing against inertia and indifference.

When Dr. Malcan retired in 2010, his successor proved more of an obstacle than an ally. Unlike her predecessor, she showed no interest in supporting the BSW program, and resistance from the Sociology and Criminal Justice faculty quickly followed. It was a sobering reality—but I was not deterred.

I had learned one thing with certainty: this role, this assignment, was not given to me by human hands—it was entrusted to me by God. And I would carry it out with resolve, knowing that both merit and faith had brought me to this place. I would not falter in the face of opposition. I was here for a purpose, and I intended to fulfill it.

CHAPTER 15

A LEGACY OF PURPOSE: TRANSFORMING LIVES THROUGH SERVICE

Building Bridges, Creating Opportunities, and Uplifting Generations

Throughout my life, one guiding truth has remained constant: purpose is not measured by individual success, but cultivated through service, leadership, and a commitment to uplifting others. Every initiative I've pursued, every project I've led, and every role I've embraced has been rooted in a belief that fulfillment comes from breaking barriers, creating pathways, and ensuring that future generations have the tools, support, and guidance they need to flourish.

During my tenure at Virginia State University, my professional journey unfolded in ways that felt divinely orchestrated —shaped by purpose, perseverance, and unwavering faith. Each accomplishment stood as a testament to the greater mission I had embraced: to empower students, strengthen communities, and build a legacy defined by service and impact. The road was not always smooth, but I stayed the course, trusting the process and knowing that every challenge and triumph was part of something greater than myself.

This journey has never been solely about personal advancement. It has been about action, advocacy, and transformation—within the halls of academia, within underserved communities, and within the very systems that call for meaningful reform. At every step, I have sought not simply to succeed, but to serve. Not merely to teach, but to inspire. And not only to lead, but to open doors wide enough for others to walk through with confidence.

A Commitment to Healthcare Access and Social Impact

In 2010, I embarked on an extraordinary mission—one that revealed the stark realities of healthcare inequality, the resilience of underserved communities, and the transformative power of collective action. I understood that healthcare is not just a privilege; it is a fundamental right. And yet, far too many people continue to lack access to basic medical services, routine care, and essential screenings that could change—or even save—their lives.

Determined to act, I recruited and joined forces with an exceptional team of colleagues, each of whom shared my commitment to service and community outreach. Together, we formed a coalition of educators and advocates, ready to meet people where they were—in spaces where need outweighed access.

I partnered with Dr. Karen Faison, Director of the Nursing Department; Dr. Ayana Conway, Assistant Professor in the Criminal Justice Department; Dr. Calton Edwards, Assistant Professor in the Mass Communication Department; and Dr. Jewel (Hairston) Bronaugh, who was then serving as Associate Administrator for the VSU Cooperative Extension.

Our team collaborated with medical professionals from the School of Medicine at Virginia Commonwealth University and traveled to

Southwest Virginia to participate in the Remote Area Medical (RAM) Health Expedition at the Wise County fairgrounds.

What we encountered there deepened our understanding of healthcare inequity in ways that no textbook, research article, or classroom discussion could ever fully convey. In Wise County, thousands of individuals relied on this temporary medical mission for care they simply could not afford elsewhere. Some had never undergone a professional medical evaluation. Others had silently endured preventable diseases, and many had waited months—some even years—for critical dental procedures, basic checkups, and diagnostic screenings.

This was not merely an event—it was their only opportunity to receive healthcare. Their only chance to be treated. Their only hope of receiving guidance for long-neglected conditions.

We immersed ourselves fully in the work, taking on roles that allowed us to interact with patients, hear their stories, and witness firsthand the inequities they faced.

Beyond medical intervention, we also addressed the vital role that nutrition plays in sustaining health and wellness. Through the VSU Cooperative Extension's mobile van, we provided fresh fruits and vegetables, reinforcing the message that healthcare is not only about treatment—but about prevention, nourishment, and holistic well-being from the inside out.

As the hours passed, we saw countless families, elderly individuals, and young children receive care that had once been out of reach. Some walked away with restored health, renewed hope, and the ability to smile again after long-needed dental work. Others left with medicine, follow-up plans, and referrals to healthcare providers who could continue their care.

What struck me most was not only the services being provided, but the **dignity being restored**. These individuals had long navigated a system that overlooked their needs—yet here, in this space, they were seen. They were heard. They were valued. They were cared for—not as statistics, but as human beings deserving of wellness and compassion.

I carried the weight of that experience with me long after the mission ended. Witnessing such disparity fueled my commitment to create sustainable programs—initiatives that would serve communities not just in crisis, but in enduring, transformative ways. It reaffirmed my belief that **education and service must always walk hand in hand**. That healthcare should be a universal right. And that lasting impact is made when we show up, when we listen, and when we act.

Through this work, I learned that service is more than a moment—it is a **commitment**, a **responsibility**, and a **promise** to never overlook the needs of the most vulnerable.

That, to me, is the true essence of bridging the gap between access and equality.

Legacy in Motion: Building a Future Beyond the Present

Legacy is not just about what we accomplish in the present; it is about ensuring that the work continues, evolves, and stands the test of time. It is the force that propels generations forward, the foundation upon which dreams are built, the torch passed from one set of hands to the next—illuminating pathways that once seemed unreachable.

Every initiative I have built, every project I have nurtured, every battle I have fought to ensure access, justice, and opportunity has been part of something far greater than myself—a mission to uplift, to empower, and to create sustainable change that will endure beyond my lifetime.

I can still feel the powerful wave of emotion that swept over me when Candace Toussaint and Stephanie Waller became the first graduates of the newly revived VSU BSW Program in 2011. That moment was more than a ceremony; it was a declaration of resilience, a testament to perseverance, a confirmation that the sacrifices made and the belief poured into rebuilding this program had been worth every challenge.

As they walked across that stage, radiating pride, confidence, and hope, I saw the future unfold before me—a future where social workers, armed with knowledge, compassion, and purpose, would step into a calling far greater than themselves. Their success was not just about earning a degree; it was about embracing a mission that would touch lives, strengthen communities, and confront systemic challenges with courage and conviction.

It was in that moment—watching their journey take flight—that I knew: this was not the destination, but the beginning of something enduring.

Legacy is not defined by the moments we witness. It is shaped by the moments yet to come: by the students who will walk through these halls in the years ahead, by the professionals who will continue the work, and by the leaders who will rise, carrying forward the mission of service and advocacy.

The journey did not stop there—and it never will

Founding of the VSU Cares Project

One year later, in 2012, another opportunity to serve emerged—one that would extend far beyond the classroom and into the heart of community care and outreach. Inspired by the RAM Healthcare Expedition in Southwest Virginia, and in collaboration with Drs. Karen Faison, Ayana Conway, and Jewel (Hairston) Bronaugh—with the support of the VSU

Board of Directors and university administrators—we established the VSU Cares Project.

This initiative was rooted in a fundamental belief: that healthcare should be accessible to all, regardless of financial status or insurance coverage. VSU Cares became a free healthcare initiative, designed to bridge the gap in medical access and provide life-changing support to uninsured and underinsured individuals.

Through strategic partnerships—including collaboration with the Virginia Dental Association Foundation's Mission of Mercy—we offered free medical screenings and dental care, ensuring that individuals in need could receive essential services, routine procedures, and preventative care.

What made VSU Cares truly extraordinary was the dedication of its volunteers: dentists, dental hygienists, doctors, nurses, social workers, and healthcare professionals who gave their time, skills, and compassion to serve those most in need.

The project quickly became a cornerstone of social impact efforts at the university, demonstrating the powerful connection between academia and real-world service. It reinforced the conviction that education and service must walk hand in hand—that knowledge must be applied for the betterment of others—and that every initiative, no matter how small, has the potential to transform lives and build a lasting legacy.

BSW Program Accreditation: A Milestone of Faith, Perseverance, and Purpose

There are moments in life that define everything that follows—turning points where determination meets opportunity, where faith carries vision forward, and where perseverance transforms dreams into reality.

For me, 2013 was one of those defining moments. After years of relentless effort, the Virginia State University (VSU) BSW Program was awarded full accreditation by the Council on Social Work Education (CSWE), an achievement that secured its place among nationally recognized and respected social work programs.

This milestone was more than institutional recognition—it was a deeply personal triumph. It reflected unwavering faith, tireless dedication, and the conviction that no dream is too distant when pursued with purpose and perseverance.

The road to accreditation was far from easy. It demanded strategic planning, exhaustive evaluations, and rigorous documentation. Every facet of the program had to meet the highest national standards. Achieving that goal required every ounce of commitment, resilience, and trust in the process.

There were moments of doubt—times when obstacles loomed large, when progress seemed elusive, when discouragement whispered that the goal might never be reached. Yet even in those moments, the vision never wavered.

Because this wasn't just about earning a credential.

This was about building a foundation for academic excellence. It was about preparing future social workers—especially those from historically marginalized communities—to step into roles as advocates, leaders, and agents of change. It was about creating access to an education that would empower students to confront injustice, uplift communities, and serve with compassion and integrity.

When accreditation was finally granted, it was more than a validation—it was a victory.

A victory for the students who had placed their trust in this program, believing that their education would equip them to lead with purpose.

A victory for the faculty who had poured their energy, passion, and belief into a vision greater than themselves.

A victory for the principle that persistence, anchored by faith, can transform visions into reality—no matter the hurdles.

I remember standing in the midst of that achievement, reflecting on the sacrifices, the long nights, the steady prayers, and the quiet moments when uncertainty pressed hard against hope. And in that moment, I understood clearly: this wasn't simply the story of a program earning accreditation.

It was the story of legacy.

It was the story of impact.

It was the story of what becomes possible when faith and perseverance walk together—when the impossible bends to the will of belief and purpose.

A Defining Moment of Growth and Legacy

In 2014, a pivotal milestone was reached—one that would permanently shape the trajectory of the Virginia State University (VSU) BSW Program. It marked the culmination of years of advocacy, sacrifice, and steadfast belief in the transformative power of social work education.

Following sustained effort and passionate leadership, the VSU Board of Visitors and the State Council of Higher Education for Virginia (SCHEV) officially approved the BSW Program's designation as a stand-alone department.

This was far more than an administrative shift—it was a moment of transformation. It affirmed that the program had not only proven its value but had established its identity and earned the autonomy to direct its own future. With departmental independence came expanded influence, deeper responsibility, and the capacity to shape the landscape of social work education with greater impact.

The approval signified that the tireless efforts invested—the late nights, the challenges, the vision pursued with unrelenting conviction—had yielded a lasting, meaningful legacy.

For years, I had devoted my energy and belief to building a program rooted in justice, service, and empowerment. I had seen firsthand the determination in students' eyes, the sense of calling that led them to this profession—not for recognition, but for purpose. I knew then, as I do now, that social work is more than a career path. It is a vocation—a calling to stand at the intersection of advocacy and action, where humanity is served, and dignity is restored.

This program was built to honor that calling. It existed to prepare students not just academically, but morally and emotionally—for the work of healing, lifting, and leading.

The decision to elevate the program to departmental status was not simply about structural change; it was about amplifying the ripple effect that would extend far beyond campus walls. Each student transformed, each professional who would go on to serve, each community strengthened by their efforts—these outcomes would all be rooted in this foundational moment.

With the approval, the BSW Program stepped out of the shadow of broader divisions and into its rightful place as a leader in social work education. It became not just a program, but a force—anchored in empowerment, dedicated to equity, and committed to service.

Reflecting on that journey—the struggles overcome, the breakthroughs hard-won—I recognized that this milestone was more than a professional achievement. It was a spiritual fulfillment. A calling answered.

It proved what I had always believed: when faith, perseverance, and purpose align, barriers dissolve, doors open, and what once seemed impossible becomes the new reality.

With that, the program entered a new era—of leadership, innovation, and impact—ready to shape the world in ways that would outlive all of

Honoring Service, Supporting Transition, and Building a Future

In 2016, I stepped into a calling that resonated deeply with my spirit—an endeavor that extended far beyond academics or curriculum design. It was a mission rooted in gratitude, responsibility, and respect for the men and women who had served our country with courage and sacrifice. This wasn't merely a policy initiative or a professional milestone—it was a promise: to walk alongside our veterans as they transitioned into civilian life, ensuring their journey was met with dignity, compassion, and understanding.

That year, I developed and secured institutional approval for the *Homefront Readjustment for the Armed Services Certificate Program*—a groundbreaking initiative designed to prepare professionals to meet the needs of veterans in transition. But the inspiration for this program wasn't found in research alone. It was born of lived experience and a powerful conversation with someone who had survived the battlefield and the return home.

That someone was Dr. Jimmie Fedrick—a 2013 graduate of the VSU BSW Program, a Purple Heart veteran, and a man who carried the weight of war and reintegration with quiet strength. When he spoke, it was with the authenticity of one who had been there—not just in the uniform, but in the shadows that often follow its removal.

Jimmie understood transition not as a logistical process, but as a deeply personal reckoning. He spoke of the emotional dislocation that came after service—how the world you return to doesn't always feel like home, how identity shifts, how pain lingers silently. He saw what others missed: the quiet battles, the unseen wounds, the systemic gaps. And with clarity and conviction, he challenged us to do better—to prepare our students, our future social workers, to truly support the veterans they would one day serve.

From that challenge, the Homefront Readjustment Certificate Program took shape. It became an academic bridge rooted in empathy and purpose, covering critical issues such as military mental health, PTSD, family reintegration, employment transitions, and the complex psychological terrain of post-service life.

But more than a curriculum, it was a shift in consciousness.

It ensured that those entering the fields of social work, education, and advocacy would no longer treat veterans as case numbers or statistics—but as people, whole and human, carrying stories that deserved to be honored and understood.

The certificate program didn't just inform—it transformed. It created space for new conversations, new competencies, and a renewed sense of collective responsibility. It underscored the essential role of social work in addressing the mental and emotional needs of military families, asserting that our veterans should never be left to navigate their healing alone.

This initiative was about more than course offerings. It was about affirming that service does not end when the uniform comes off—and neither should our support.

It was about honoring sacrifice not just with medals, but with meaningful, sustained care.

And most of all, it was about building a future where every veteran is seen, heard, and empowered to thrive.

A Vision for Growth and Impact

Under the visionary leadership of Dr. Donald Palm, Provost of Virginia State University, a transformative mission began to take shape—one that would expand the reach and deepen the impact of social work education on campus and beyond. That year marked the genesis of the Master of Social Work (MSW) Program, an initiative rooted not only in academic advancement but in a profound commitment to social responsibility and human dignity.

Dr. Palm's leadership was marked by both strategic foresight and sincere compassion. He recognized the urgent and growing need for highly trained social work professionals capable of addressing the complex realities of inequality, mental health challenges, and systemic injustice. His clarity of purpose helped illuminate a path forward—one that connected institutional growth with meaningful societal change.

With careful planning, strong advocacy, and an unshakable belief in the power of social work to heal, transform, and empower, we began laying the foundation for what would become a vital and enduring program. The MSW initiative was not simply an expansion of curriculum; it was a bold promise to the future—a declaration that VSU was committed to preparing leaders who would reform policy, champion equity, and amplify the voices of those too often left unheard.

In that pivotal moment, I felt the certainty of purpose settle over us. We were not just creating a graduate program—we were planting seeds of lasting impact, building something that would outlive us, serve communities far and wide, and shape generations of compassionate, justice-driven leaders.

A Journey of Cultural Immersion, Service, and Legacy

In 2017, I embarked on one of the most transformative experiences of my career—an initiative that expanded perspectives, deepened cultural understanding, and underscored the vital role of global service in social work education. Alongside Dr. Maxine Sample, Director of the VSU George Bennett International Education Department, and Jane Parker, Director of Field Education for the Social Work Department, we launched the faculty-led Study Abroad Program to Ghana.

But this was more than an academic endeavor—it was a mission rooted in human connection, cross-cultural advocacy, and experiential learning. Our goal was to create a bridge between cultures and to provide students with firsthand insight into global social work practice.

I wanted students to step beyond the confines of textbooks and classroom discussions—to see, feel, and engage with the lived realities of individuals and communities across the globe. Social work, after all, is not merely a discipline of theory—it is a discipline of empathy, systems navigation, and cultural awareness. It is a commitment to understanding how history, heritage, and social context shape the health and resilience of families and communities.

This journey challenged our students to stretch beyond their comfort zones. It guided them into spaces where they could witness the essence of service and intercultural exchange, not as abstract ideas, but as living truths. What they encountered in Ghana was not just a glimpse of another world—it was a powerful reminder that meaningful change begins with understanding, humility, and human connection.

A Journey of Reflection, Connection, and Legacy

In 2019, I embarked on a two-month sabbatical that took me deep into the heart of Ghana—a land rich with history, vibrancy, and an unshakable sense of community. From the moment my feet touched Ghanaian soil, I was enveloped in a warmth that felt ancestral, as if I were returning to something deeply familiar. The rhythm of daily life moved through bustling villages and sunlit marketplaces, where resilience blossomed amid economic hardship and hope thrived in even the simplest moments.

I sat with local leaders, educators, and service workers whose stories of perseverance left an indelible imprint on my spirit. Their words echoed a universal truth: no matter where we come from, our humanity binds us. Each shared meal, each conversation revealed the depth of that connection—and reaffirmed that education and service must transcend borders, generations, and circumstances.

That journey awakened something within me. It wove together years of mentorship, advocacy, and cultural exchange into a living testament of purpose and possibility. From that awakening, the **Dr. Gwendolyn Thornton Endowment Scholarship** was born—a bridge built from conviction and vision, rooted in the belief that knowledge is a sacred inheritance to be passed forward.

Through this scholarship, students are not only supported—they are called. Called to rise, to learn, to serve. Each step they take toward justice, healing, and leadership carries the heartbeat of this mission.

This is more than a legacy. It is a living force—active, enduring, and ever-reaching—moving through the lives it touches, generation after generation

A Legacy of Service and Global Impact

In 2020, as global instability deepened and communities worldwide faced profound uncertainty, my colleague Jane Parker and I responded to a call that could no longer be confined to the classroom. Together, we founded **Mimosa International Foundation of America, Inc.**, a 501(c)(3) nonprofit born of urgency, compassion, and the unwavering belief that humanity deserves better.

Years of mentoring social work students had prepared me to teach advocacy and care—but what was unfolding, particularly across parts of Africa, demanded more than theory. It demanded action. Communities in Ghana and beyond weren't just enduring hardship—they were fighting for their futures.

Mimosa became our vessel for change, a bridge connecting continents through initiatives grounded in equity, empowerment, and culturally responsive service. From health and wellness programs to economic development projects and mentorship rooted in shared heritage, we began creating opportunities in places where few had existed before.

The work was not without its challenges. Resources were limited, logistics were complex, and progress often felt painstakingly slow. But each story we encountered, each life we touched, reaffirmed our mission. We weren't just offering aid—we were building solidarity.

From remote villages to global advocacy platforms, Mimosa's reach grew, transforming service into a powerful expression of unity. This is more than legacy. It is a **living testament**—proof that when hearts and hands unite across borders, lasting change is not only possible, it is inevitable.

CHAPTER 16

WALKING IN DIVINE ORDER: TRUSTING GOD'S PLAN THROUGH LIFE'S TRANSITION

Navigating Loss, Trusting Faith

Throughout my tenure at Virginia State University—amid the achievements, milestones, and moments of triumph—I came to understand a truth that reached far beyond professional success: the unmistakable presence of God's divine order, His preparation, and His unwavering faithfulness.

Life taught me that growth, achievement, and purpose do not exist apart from faith—they walk alongside it. Even as my career blossomed, I found myself navigating deep personal transitions, learning to surrender fully to God's plan, even when it tested my heart, challenged my spirit, and stretched my understanding of what the future might hold.

Our journey through life is not measured solely by the years we are given, but by the legacy of love, wisdom, and faith we leave behind. Through every changing season, we are called to embrace the divine process—trusting that even in sorrow, God's plan continues to unfold with perfect intention, leading us gently into His eternal embrace.

A Century of Faith: Granny's Unwavering Trust in God's Promise

One of the most profound moments during this period of my life was standing beside my grandmother, Coreine—lovingly known as Granny—as she completed the earthly chapter of her journey.

Granny was the eldest of Nana and Papa's children, and from her mid-forties onward, she carried an unshakable belief in a promise she said God had given her: that she would live to see her 100th birthday. And, as always, He fulfilled His word.

On September 11, 2011, family and friends gathered to honor that promise, celebrating her century of life at Second Baptist Church on Idlewood Avenue in Richmond, Virginia, where she had faithfully worshiped for over seventy years.

It was an occasion marked by joy, reverence, and deep gratitude—a fitting tribute to a life defined by faith, service, and quiet wisdom.

Just months later, I received a call that signaled the next phase of her journey. Granny had simply stopped eating—a peaceful, intentional surrender to the process God had set before her.

Without hesitation, I left VSU. I knew this was a moment that required my presence, my love, and an open heart. On February 24, 2012, I sat by her side, holding her hand, ensuring she knew she was not alone.

As I watched her begin to drift toward another realm, a wave of emotion overcame me. It wasn't a lack of trust in the process—it was the sheer weight of witnessing something so sacred, so absolute.

For a moment, fear gripped me. My thoughts raced: *Oh my God, my grandmother is going to leave this world, and I am all alone with her.*

Then, in the stillness, a presence greater than my fear settled over me. I heard, as clearly as if it had been spoken aloud: *"Peace, be still. Know that I am God. I am here with you."*

In that instant, fear was replaced by peace, by certainty, and by the understanding that this moment was not mine to carry alone—it was already being held by God.

I gently read Psalm 23 aloud, letting the familiar words fill the room, surrounding Granny with the same faith she had lived by for a century. I told her it was okay to go, that God was waiting, and that we would be alright.

As I spoke, I felt her spirit hover for a brief, weightless moment—then ascend. It was indescribable, a passing from one dimension into the next.

It was in that moment that I fully grasped the beauty of God's process. It is not meant to be resisted or feared, but to be walked through with obedience and trust. Some moments bring sorrow, but even in sorrow, there is purpose. Some goodbyes are earthly, but they are never final.

Through Granny's life, her faith, and the dignity with which she surrendered to God's will, I learned that letting go is not the end. It is a passage into something greater. Her legacy—her unwavering belief, her quiet strength—remains with me in every step I take.

And so, I continue forward, trusting, surrendering, and walking in divine order—exactly as God intended.

Life reminds us that while we walk in purpose, faith, and love, we are never truly prepared for the transitions that come. We hold tight to the ones we love, we cherish their presence, and when the time comes for them to step into eternity, we must learn to balance grief with trust in God's perfect plan.

The journey of loss is not only one of mourning—it is one of reflection, resilience, and steadfast faith. Though we miss their physical presence, their spirit, their love, and their lessons remain eternally woven into the fabric of our lives.

A Full Circle: Embracing the Next Chapter with Grace and Purpose

In 2021, Virginia State University extended an early retirement package, and deep within my spirit, I felt an undeniable pull, an unshakable knowing that the time had come. At 70 years old, I had given my all, poured my heart into every student, every lesson, every challenge, and every triumph. This was more than a career, it was a calling, a divine purpose fulfilled at this juncture of my life's journey.

The decision was not made lightly. I sat with it, prayed over it, and reflected on the seasons that had shaped me. I could feel the weight of countless memories pressing against my heart—the long nights of preparation, the victories of students who flourished under my guidance, the quiet moments when I knew I had made a difference. And so, with a deep breath and a full heart, I turned in my letter of resignation, passing the torch to Dr. Jimmie Fedrick, trusting that he would carry the legacy forward with integrity and vision.

Then came May 12, 2023, a day filled with emotion, reflection, and an overwhelming sense of completion. I took my final walk down the aisle at VSU, surrounded by the energy of the Class of 1973, celebrating our 50-year reunion. As I stood among them, I could feel the weight of my journey, the winding roads, the setbacks, the triumphs.

I had not graduated with my cohort in 1973. Life had taken me down a different path, one fraught with detours, but also with invaluable lessons.

Yet here I was, standing in this moment, a testimony to perseverance. From a college dropout to a department chair. From uncertainty to leadership. And now, as I bid farewell to this chapter, I was honored with the 2020-2021 Provost Outstanding Faculty Award and Professor Emeritus status—recognitions of not just my accomplishments, but of the unwavering spirit that had carried me through the decades.

This was not just a transition; it was a full circle moment. It was the divine affirmation that every challenge, every tear, every sacrifice had been part of a greater purpose. And as I stepped forward into the unknown, I did so with faith, knowing that when one door closes, another opens—not by chance, but by God's divine design.

CHAPTER 17

FOLLOW THE PROCESS

Walking in Purpose, Leaving a Legacy

I have walked through this life with faith as my compass—sometimes steady, sometimes trembling, but always present. It was never blind belief; it was rooted, lived, and weathered. That same faith held me when everything else felt uncertain. It whispered "trust" when logic faltered and guided my steps when the path disappeared beneath me. I followed the process not because I saw the finish line—but because my spirit recognized the rhythm of becoming.

Perseverance became the pulse beneath my feet. Even when doors closed, even when disappointment knocked the breath from my body, I refused to stop. The world tried to rewrite my story, but I held the pen. I kept walking—with swollen feet, a heavy heart, and a soul determined to rise. Persistence, to me, is sacred. It means honoring the journey even when it makes no sense, trusting that breakthrough lives just beyond the breaking.

Realness and authenticity saved me. It called me back to myself when the world asked me to perform. It taught me to speak honestly, to love without masks, and to stand tall in rooms that tried to shrink me. I never sought to be polished—I sought to be whole. Truth became my armor. And from that truth, I offered others something real to hold on to—something unshaken by pretense.

Openness stretched me. It turned fear into a doorway. Life showed up with changes I didn't ask for, and I chose not to resist them. I let them shape me. Every detour, every surprise, every room I entered felt like divine choreography. Openness made me soft enough to grow, strong enough to serve, and wise enough to pour into others without losing myself.

Compassion became the balm I didn't know I needed. It softened my edges and expanded my heart. Through it, I discovered that leadership is not about control—it is about care. Power doesn't flow from titles; it pours from kindness. Compassion held my hand when I needed it, and gave me the courage to extend that same hand to someone else.

Empathy became my bridge. It allowed me to cross into the hearts of others and see the world through their eyes. It reminded me to listen with intention, to love without agenda, and to hold space without needing to fix. My own pain became a point of connection—a way to remind others that healing is possible, and that they are never alone.

Support—oh, how it carried me. I remember the prayers whispered when I had no words left. The friends who sat with me in silence. The hands that held me—not because I asked, but because they knew I needed it. Those sacred bonds are stitched into the fabric of my life. To every soul who stood beside me—thank you. You were God's grace in human form.

And service?

Service has always been my sanctuary. I was never drawn to applause—but to the quiet work of lifting others. To me, legacy isn't built on recognition—it is built on impact. On presence. On offering your gifts and trusting that they will ripple beyond your reach. That is the joy I have found. That is the life I have lived.

Now, as I prepare to turn the page, I feel both the ache and the awe of what comes next. My journey isn't just mine—it belongs to every heart that walks beside me, every reader who finds solace or strength in these words, and every seeker still searching for light.

So, if you are holding this book, hear me:

Follow the process. Trust the mystery. Stay faithful to what feels true.

Be honest. Be kind. Be open.

Let compassion shape you. Let resilience carry you. Lift someone as you rise.

And when the time comes for your story to be told—make it one that glows with grace, leaves footprints of hope, and lives far beyond the final page.

Because when you live this way, your life will be filled with light—and it will never be lived in vain.

Gratitude: A Life Touched by Many

I would not be here without the unwavering support of those who have stood by me. To my village—family, friends, colleagues, mentors, students, and clients—you have shaped my journey in ways I could never fully express. You poured into me, strengthened me, and uplifted me.

I thank God for guiding me every step of the way—for placing the right people in my life at the right time, for giving me the strength to endure, the wisdom to lead, and the humility to serve.

As I step forward into this next phase, I do so with peace, with gratitude, and with the deep certainty that my work here has not been in vain.

Following God's Process

Through every transition and each sacred goodbye, I have come to understand that loss is not an ending—it is an invitation to feel the lasting presence of those we've loved. Their spirit remains with us, woven into the fabric of our days.

Even when grief presses heavily on my heart, when sorrow lingers at the edges of quiet moments, I lean into the truth I've come to know: God's process is never wrong. We may not always understand it, but we can trust that every step is part of His divine plan, unfolding in perfect time.

Love does not die. It moves with us—it lifts, it holds, it strengthens. It reminds us that transition isn't about parting, but becoming. And in that sacred knowing, I press forward, memory by memory, trusting that every farewell is guiding us closer to something greater—to His eternal embrace.

A Final Blessing

May your footsteps be guided by faith—steady through the valleys, bold upon the peaks.

May you find strength in every trial, and tenderness in every lesson. May love root itself in all you do—the kind that heals, uplifts, and multiplies.

May your voice carry forward the stories that matter, and your light stretch beyond what eyes can see.

You were never meant to walk easy roads, but you were always meant to rise.

And as you go, may your legacy—woven with courage, grace, and truth—bless generations to come.

Amen.

THE SEEDS I CARRIED: A LEGACY IN BLOOM

The lantern I once carried into the hallways of learning still glows—though now, it is held by others.

My journey began in a rural village, shaped by early struggles and the quiet strength found in a one-room schoolhouse. Faith grew with me, deepening through every chapter. I learned to teach not only from textbooks, but from the lived texture of my own experience—woven with resilience, grace, and a growing understanding of what once felt unfamiliar.

When my understanding of God shifted, it wasn't through thunderclaps or revelation. It happened in the stillness of leadership, in classrooms illuminated by curiosity, and in conversations where questions were welcomed like prayers. My faith became a living dialogue. As I matured into the fullness of my educational and professional life, my relationship with the church evolved as well—no longer just a sanctuary, but a space of spiritual stewardship and communal accountability.

Now, I see the seeds of that journey blooming all around me. The initiatives I helped spark continue to bear fruit—not merely through plaques or programs, but through people: in how they teach, how they lead, how they listen. If I could visit myself during those pivotal moments of doubt and uncertainty, I would simply say: You are becoming. Don't rush grace. Trust and follow the shaping.

And the next generation? They have taken up the work with vision and vigor. Some lead with boldness, others with stories or acts of quiet courage. They carry forward the values I lived—not through imitation, but through transformation—bringing their own brilliance to spaces I could never have reached alone.

The most enduring legacy is not the path I walked, but the footprints I left for others to follow—and the light they now carry into their own journeys.

My former BSW students and mentees - Dr. Jimmie Fedrick, Dr. Brittany Short and Mr. Daryl Simmons - now faculty members and in leadership positions at VSU

Christian-Carter-Brown Ancestral Village

Tribute to the descendants of Ida and William Christian (Nana and Papa)

Coreine Christian

Alice Christian-Brown

Idabelle Christian-Hayden

Ruth Christian-Henderson

Harold Christian

Harriet 'Sis' Christian

Martha Christian-Armstead

Louberta 'Bert' Christian-Jones

Mary 'Lois' Christian-Green

Virginia 'Tweedie Weedie'
Christian-Jones

Mary Frances Hill

William 'Bill' Armstead, Sr

Joan Christian-Turnage

Erselle Armstead-Robinson

Alice 'Shortie' Armsted-Jamerson

Robert 'Al' Hayden

Marilyn 'Mousie' Christian-Fenner   Benjamin 'Bennie' Lockley

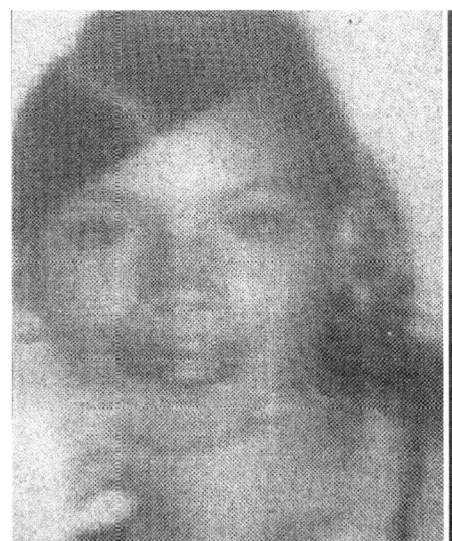

Waynette Fenner-Simmons   William 'Junnie' Armstead, Jr

Clothelda 'Mookie' Hill   Timothy 'Tim' Hill, Sr

Timothy 'TJ' Hill, Jr

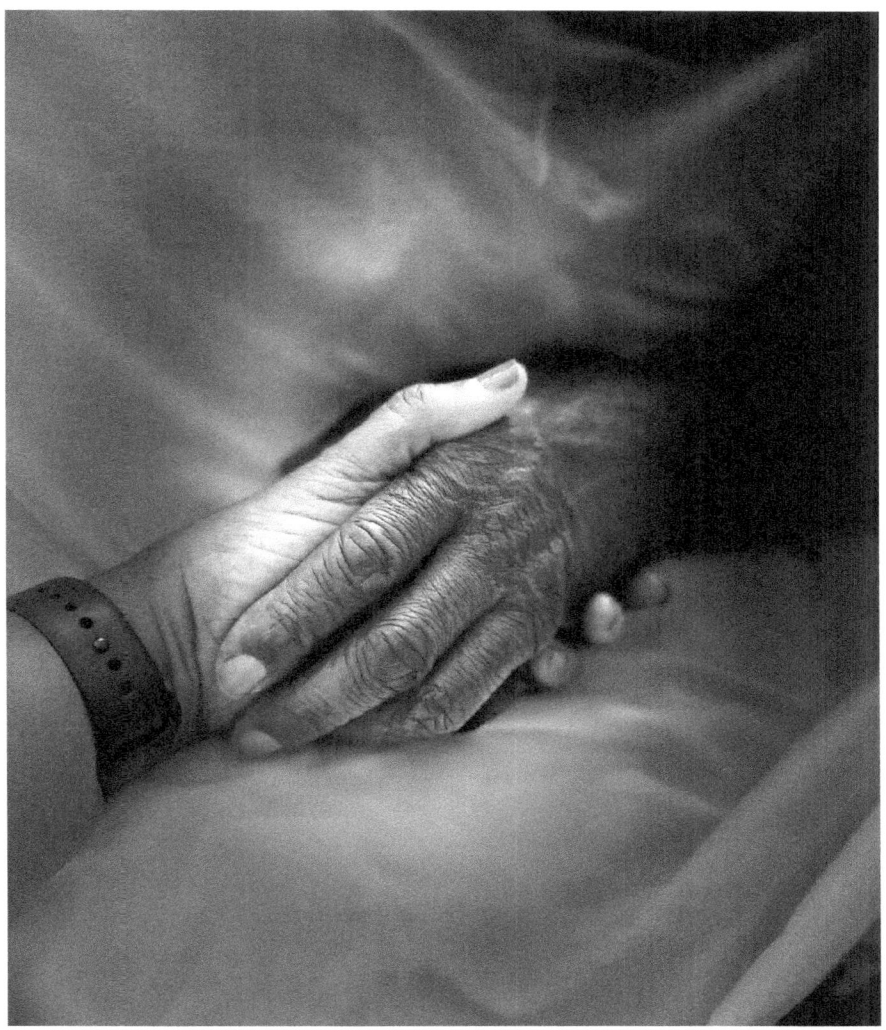

Dr. Glasgow holding my hand as he was in the stage of transition - symbolic
of passing the ancestral blessings
(Inspiration for my book cover)

ABOUT THE AUTHOR

Dr. Gwendolyn Brown-Thornton's journey began in a close-knit, rural Virginia community—a modern echo of ancestral African village life, rich in faith, kinship, and tradition. Educated in a segregated one-room schoolhouse during the civil rights era, she emerged with a deep reverence for the Queen Mothers, spiritual guides, and village fathers whose wisdom and sacrifice shaped her path. As an educator, mentor, and legacy keeper, Dr. Thornton carries their voices forward—offering audiences a tapestry of resilience, cultural pride, and generational healing. Her life's work honors unsung heroes and kindles hope in those called to teach, uplift, and transform.